How to Survive   *'re an Adult*

"With mastery and   a journey from the identity we constructed to protect us as children to authentic adults living a creative, meaningful, and joyful life."   **— Allan Badiner,** editor of *Zig Zag Zen* and *Mindfulness in the Marketplace*

"As a yoga teacher of thirty-seven years, whose chronological age (almost seventy) belies his emotional age (on the best of days about thirteen), I found Ira Israel's book enormously helpful in suggesting a number of simple ways that I might finally learn to act my actual age. I especially enjoyed his take on dharma and our proper place in the grand scheme of things, which is perhaps the most lucid I've ever encountered on that difficult subject."
    — Richard Rosen, author of *Yoga FAQ* and *The Yoga of Breath*

"Ira Israel shares his wealth of knowledge to help us better understand ourselves, our behaviors, and most importantly the tools to live fully, happily, and authentically. This book is a gift."
    — Zippora Karz, author of *The Sugarless Plum* and former New York City Ballet soloist

"Ira Israel is a modern-day prophet — an amazing teacher, thinker, and leader whose work seamlessly combines philosophy, spirituality, and psychology. Read this book and be transformed."
    — Rabbi Joshua Buchin

"Chock-full of valuable wisdom that will benefit just about any reader who has ever struggled with issues of approval, which probably includes about 98 percent of the population. I recommend it highly!"
    — Linda Bloom, LCSW, coauthor of *101 Things I Wish I Knew When I Got Married*

"Ira Israel has discovered the way to be fully mature and keep a childlike sense of wonder."   **— Sam Keen,** author of *Fire in the Belly*

"We all want to be strong adults, yet at the same time, deep down, we want to be taken care of. Reconciling this is the task, and this book is up to the task. I highly recommend it."
    — Dr. Adam Sheck, director of Los Angeles Counseling Center

"A helpful guide for the treatment of stress, anxiety, and depression stemming from painful childhood events. Ira Israel's unique and progressive vision will help people overcome afflictions and addictions so that they may live healthier, more authentic, and successful lives."
— **Shannon Byrnes,** licensed marriage and family therapist

"With this comprehensive and engaging book, Ira Israel stations himself on the cutting edge where modern psychology meets authentic spirituality.... Illuminating and transformational."
— **Philip Goldberg,** author of *American Veda* and *Roadsigns*

"Ira Israel has given us a tremendous gift in his new book! His wisdom, clarity, and insight permeate seamlessly through the pages in service to us all living in a greater landscape of joy and truth. A must-read for all truth seekers on the path."
— **Govind Das**

"A practical guide to identifying the impact you're allowing your childhood wounds to have on yourself and your relationships in business and in life."
— **Kenneth Borg,** CEO of The Social Life

"Prepare to shake up your psyche with *How to Survive Your Childhood Now That You're an Adult.* What author Ira Israel offers is an energizing breath of fresh air for those whose childhoods have left them dulled and sleepwalking through life. This book will help you overcome fears and jump with both feet into the authentic self that is waiting for you!"
— **Donald Altman,** America's Mindfulness Coach and bestselling author of *Clearing Emotional Clutter* and *One-Minute Mindfulness*

"Ira Israel is a brilliant author. His book has us examine ourselves and our cultural paradigm through the lens of psychology and spirituality. He gives us tools to find our authentic selves. I highly recommend this book."
— **Denise Wiesner, LAc,** author of *The Conception of Love*

"Ira Israel is a deep thinker, always researching and pondering the human condition, and such a good writer that the heady musings in *How to Survive Your Childhood Now That You're an Adult* are presented in a thoroughly entertaining fashion (that may also help the inquiring reader put some of the world's craziness into better focus). A joy to read."
— **Gill Holland,** producer

"Ira Israel is a brilliant, progressive teacher who draws upon philosophical and psychological teachings from Buddhism and Hinduism as well as Western psychology and thought in order to find the lessons we need to learn today to embody authenticity and experience true happiness. This book is the guide we have all been looking for to navigate the complexities of the mind in the modern world."

— **Felicia Tomasko**, editor in chief of *LA Yoga*
and *Boston Yoga* magazines

"If you are looking for new ways to see old problems, I recommend this book." — **Geeta Novotny**, award-winning vocalist
and creator of Revolution Voice™

"If there is one thing you will learn from Ira Israel's inspiring and transformative book it is that you are your own agent of change and you can achieve an authentic life. It may be hard work to find your path and stay on it, but finding out who you must be and being that person ('mitigating hypocrisy,' as he says) is your best shot at lasting happiness." — **Emmanuel Itier**, director

"An engaging and thoughtful book. Integrating psychology, philosophy, meditation, and common sense with discernment, Ira Israel guides the reader skillfully to authenticity and happiness."

— **Frederic Luskin, PhD**, author of *Forgive for Good*

"A masterful and most relevant book for our times. Highly recommended!" — **Larry Payne, PhD**, founding director of
Yoga Therapy Rx™ and coauthor of *Yoga for Dummies*

"Ira Israel's psychological insights into the causes of depression and anxiety are staggering, and his writing is poignant and provocative. I'm going to recommend this book to many patients."

— **Jenny Pascal**, licensed marriage and family therapist

"A great read to provide you with a new view for forging a more expansive future and allowing you to let go of the past."

— **Ronald Alexander, PhD**, author *Wise Mind, Open Mind*
and executive director of Open Mind Training Institute

"Ira Israel shows us the steps in experiencing the truth of who and what we are. I highly recommend this book as a guide to authenticity and well-being." — **Elliott S. Dacher, MD,** author of *Aware, Awake, Alive*

"This fiercely compassionate book offers us a deep excavation to exhume the authentic self, experience the authentic relationship, and break the chain of suffering in our toxic society."
— **Julie J. Morley,** environmental educator and author of *Spirit Walk* and *Sacred Future*

"Ira Israel's courageous, iconic, and riveting new book takes on the status quo: it illuminates our society's extremely narrow bandwidth for emotions. He helps the reader realize the power of the loving and genuine relationships that enable access to the true self. This is a very brave book by someone with an eagle eye and an open and tremendous heart."
— **Dr. Joanne Cacciatore,** author of *Bearing the Unbearable* and founder of MISS Foundation

"Ira Israel is a powerhouse of insight and guidance!"
— **Dr. Janeane Bernstein, EdD,** host of *Get the Funk Out!*

"One of the lies being perpetuated in the name of meditation is that you need to be submissive and spiritual in order to practice. In other words, develop a false self and meditate as that. The truth is the opposite: be your naturally defiant and wild self, and discover the serenity in being real. Ira Israel is challenging a whole army of these crippling, imprisoning assumptions that people are being told to impose upon themselves." — **Lorin Roche, PhD,** author of *The Radiance Sutras*

"Ira Israel draws upon a broad and deep array of knowledge to brilliantly expand the paradigm of mindfulness by making us conscious of everything we absorb unconsciously in culture. Few thinkers give us more tools to guide us through the minefield preceding personal empowerment than Ira." — **Warren Farrell, PhD,** author of *The Myth of Male Power*

HOW TO SURVIVE YOUR CHILDHOOD NOW THAT YOU'RE AN ADULT

HOW TO SURVIVE YOUR CHILDHOOD NOW THAT YOU'RE AN ADULT

A Path to Authenticity and Awakening

IRA ISRAEL

Foreword by Katherine Woodward Thomas

New World Library
Novato, California

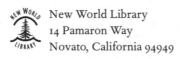

New World Library
14 Pamaron Way
Novato, California 94949

The material in this book is intended for education. It is not meant to take the place of diagnosis and treatment by a qualified medical practitioner or therapist. No expressed or implied guarantee of the effects of the use of the recommendations can be given or liability taken.

Text design by Tona Pearce Myers

Library of Congress Cataloging-in-Publication data is available.

First printing, November 2017
ISBN 978-1-60868-507-3
Ebook ISBN 978-1-60868-508-0

Printed in Canada on 100% postconsumer-waste recycled paper

New World Library is proud to be a Gold Certified Environmentally Responsible Publisher. Publisher certification awarded by Green Press Initiative. www.greenpressinitiative.org

10   9   8   7   6   5   4   3   2   1

Dedicated to Doctor Thomas Rodda

It is better to be hated for what you are than loved for what you are not.

— ANDRÉ GIDE

Contents

Foreword

S o many of our brightest teachers today speak of enlightenment — both personal and planetary — from the moun-
taintop of their own awakened state. Benevolently enticing us
toward the possibility of being deeply present in the eternal
now, expanding into unconditional love for ourselves and others, and awakening to a blissful oneness with all of life. Yet as
much as we may yearn for these experiences, for most of us, it's
as if Fred Astaire were dancing in topcoat and tails, effortlessly
gliding around the dance floor and saying with a big toothy
grin, "Just dance like this."

While it might be hard to admit, for most of us, the "maya"
in which we live — otherwise known as the cluster of cultural
norms, assumptions, and expectations we automatically pledge
allegiance to at a very young age (as well as the goals that often
accompany them) — will not dissolve simply because we take
up meditating for twenty minutes each morning, study to become a yoga teacher, or take a three-week hike through the
Himalayas. These covert and pervasive assumptions must be
made visible, challenged, and consciously evolved with great
intelligence and dogged devotion, so that we might renew our

mind-set to discover deeper, more authentic, and more life-affirming truths by which to live.

The cultural illusions that Ira Israel so elegantly unpacks in this deep-thinking dive into the heart of being human are nothing short of a revelation. Finally, we have a name for that which has been driving us to be so driven. We understand, perhaps for the very first time, the real reasons that record numbers of us are struggling with an insidious low-grade fever of depression and anxiety. Yet more importantly, we begin to glimpse ways to move beyond the sea of discontent that so many of us have been swimming in, to reclaim the joy of what it is to be fully alive, and to live with a deeper sense of relatedness to one another and to all of life.

Over my many years of teaching, I have discovered that there are basically two ways in which we human beings grow. One is that we grow horizontally. This means that we grow within the system we are already steeped in. For example, if you believe yourself to live in a dog-eat-dog world, and you spend your days trying to increase your skills in the hopes of becoming the leader of the pack, then horizontal growth might be learning how to be a bigger, better barker. Or learning to run faster so you can leave the other "dogs" in the dust. In other words, horizontal growth is about learning new skills and growing new capacities to master the current world you already inhabit.

However, there is also such a thing as vertical growth — growth that challenges, and even deconstructs, our current worldview and awakens us to another perspective altogether. It might be the sudden awareness that if you begin cooperating rather than competing with the other "dogs," you just might be able to increase the well-being and happiness of the entire tribe of canines. This kind of growth creates radical and lasting change for the better. It's the moment when Dorothy leaves her black-and-white world and suddenly finds herself immersed in a brilliantly colorful one, or when Helen Keller first comprehends "wa wa" (water) in a gasp of illumination. For the very first time, all you thought you knew is no longer relevant, and you realize in an instant that life will never be the same again! Everything is now radically repositioned and up for review inside your new perspective.

This unique and transformative book is a catalyst for vertical growth, inviting us to question long-held cultural assumptions about life and love that may no longer be relevant and that may even be doing us harm. It is a compelling conversation that promises to unleash greater levels of well-being, happiness, authenticity, and depth in all of our relationships.

So if Ira pulls the rug out from under your feet and obliges you to set aside your certainty in favor of what you don't even know that you don't yet know, fear not. His mission is clear. He is devoted to waking us from our collective confusion and setting us on a more wholesome pathway so that we can find our way home to our own true north, and closer to the hearts of one another.

Helping us to grow up, in more ways than one.

— Katherine Woodward Thomas,
New York Times–bestselling author of
Calling in "The One" and *Conscious Uncoupling*

Introduction

Every adult wants to live a version of what he or she imagines is "the good life." However, our versions of "the good life" are not only culturally contingent but typically also intense amalgams of reactions to the approval and disapproval that we received as children. Many people have default voices in their heads that tell them that whatever they do is not good enough. This hedonic treadmill manifests as phrases such as "I'll be happy when I have a better...home, job, relationship, salary, vacation, automobile." The origin of this voice is the wounded child inside of us subconsciously and retroactively seeking the acceptance, approval, and love of primary caregivers (parents, teachers, siblings, and so on) who withheld love, loved us *conditionally*, or treated us in ways we did not understand. As sentient beings, we primarily desire one thing above all: *to be loved unconditionally*. But we grew up in a highly competitive, scarcity-based society that provided us with tools to gain love *conditionally* — because we are talented, good-looking, go to good schools, get good grades, write well, speak well, dress well, earn boatloads of money, take vacations in the most exclusive places, and so on.

Children create "false selves" — facades, personas — in order to obtain the acceptance, approval, and love they crave; however, any acceptance, approval, or "love" that we receive as adults based on our facades, and not on our inner and usually somewhat messy authentic selves, ultimately causes resentment. Many people have become so closely identified with their facades that they no longer know who they are, other than what it says on their business cards, résumés, Facebook or LinkedIn profiles, Instagram and Twitter accounts, or in Google searches. Some younger people even judge or score their lives daily by the quantity of social media followers they have.

Over 20 million Americans take antidepressants every day. Consider the possibility that the problem Americans face is not some rogue gene for depression. Our definition of depression might be culturally contingent. Maybe what we are experiencing is really loneliness, or the inability to connect with and securely attach to fellow human beings, thinly veiled as pathology? Or maybe it is an inner feeling of unlovableness that was inadvertently inculcated into us by our parents and school system continually prodding us to be more, better, different?

Many people in my generation, through the iconography and symbolism of popular-culture songs, films, television programs, and books, were tacitly promised the American dream: if you do well in school, then you will land a great job, marry a wonderful person, have exceptional kids, live in a fabulous house, and be happy. Many of my peers accomplished the school/job/marriage/kids/house part of that equation and are still not happy. Actually they feel betrayed — mostly because those school/job/marriage/kids/house formulas are deathly expensive and force them to work eighty hours a week just to maintain a particular lifestyle.

How to Survive Your Childhood Now That You're an Adult: A Path to Authenticity and Awakening provides explanations as well as practical tools to help you live the life you truly want and be happy. Chapters 1 through 6 explore our level of awareness about subconscious beliefs or assumptions so that we can get some insight into our "way of being" in the world, how we choose to present ourselves to others, our attachment styles, the ways we think about work, and the activities we use to blow off steam. The goal is to raise our level of awareness about things that may be automatic, review the matrices of assumptions that construct our realities, and choose to make the healthiest decisions possible. We need to be cognizant of how prejudices and fears built during childhood may influence our adult decisions. To do this, we will examine the unwitting psychological ramifications of capitalism, science, and religion. I hope this book provides different ways of seeing some of the ideas and conventions that we as a culture consider to be "normal."

One of the wonderful things about the growing trend of mindfulness (Buddhism lite, as I call it) in our culture is that people learn to observe their thoughts without identifying with them. And once we take the first steps on the path to awakening, we often notice that many of the characteristics we developed in order to get our emotional and psychological needs met as children are now hindering us from getting the love we desire as adults. We all learned how to get admired, but do we know how to be loving, lovable, loved?

The first chapter of this book deconstructs what we think of as authenticity, and the following chapters raise consciousness concerning the ways of being in the world that we created to get our emotional and psychological needs met as children as best we could. In this book we examine the myriad factors that influence the thousands of thoughts we experience every day. In particular, I argue that the dynamics of our earlier relationships with our primary caregivers, our society's myth regarding romance and romantic love, and the hypercompetitiveness of our version of capitalism have profound effects on the way we think, feel, and interact with others. Chapters 7 through 11 will lead you toward a reconstruction and give you tools to create a fresh perspective on who you are and what type of life you want to create — so that you can live as authentically and as "awake" as possible. Specifically, I advocate creating a new definition of authenticity, one that encapsulates attachment, atonement, attunement, presence, and congruence.

In my study of consciousness during the past thirty years, I have aggregated an array of tools for alleviating suffering and keeping people at the higher end of their happiness spectrums. The number one thing that correlates with happiness is how we connect with and attach to other people. Human beings are interdependent creatures. We do not grow or evolve in bubbles. We want and need our connections to other people to be secure, trustworthy, positive, supportive, loving, and healthy. But we live in a culture that inadvertently foments separation and alienation — namely, by putting us in constant competition with other people as workers, money earners, and consumers — and so we lead unbalanced lives, sometimes double lives, and fall prey to afflictions and addictions.

The only solution is authenticity, which is difficult but must be attempted and practiced daily. As the saying goes, we must "be the change we want to see in the world." It is up to us to break the chains of unskillful solutions that were handed down to us, such as constructing glitzy and cool facades. We must consciously decide who we want to be, what type of relationships will nourish us, and what type of world we want to live in. Making commitments to healthy practices such as meditation and yoga, and being congruent — having our outer lives match our inner lives — will keep us at the higher ends of our happiness spectrums.

In this book we:

- explore how to surf the apparent paradoxes of life.
- learn how to be present.
- learn how to embrace every moment of our lives.
- discover how to shed fears and prejudices.
- learn how to have discipline.
- recognize our attachment styles and learn how to improve them.
- discern what activities we use to blow off steam and stop them from becoming afflictions or addictions.
- learn how to attune to other people so that we can securely connect with them.
- learn how to be okay with the fact that our futures are uncertain, and that, when they occur, they will certainly contain both joys and sorrows.

Chapter 1

What Does It Mean to Be Authentic?

When someone tells me that he wishes to be authentic with me, my body tenses up as if it were about to be stabbed. Usually what the person means is that he wants to be brutally honest with me (emphasis on *brutally*), he imagines that what he wants to say is going to offend me, and he thinks that I will be more receptive and that it will somehow soften the blow if he claims that his comment falls under the pretense of "being authentic." This perception is inaccurate. Most people would not know authenticity if it bit them on the leg.

What then is authenticity? Colloquially, "being authentic" usually describes someone sincerely speaking his deep inner thoughts, a supposedly honest monologue, one that is often critical about something emotionally stinging or at least sensitive, and marginally beyond the scope of what we consider to be normal, acceptable, or polite everyday conversation. You would not say to someone: "I want to be authentic with you: I think it is going to rain." Most often people say things such as: "I need to be authentic with you: this relationship is not working for me anymore." Or: "Boss, I don't feel that business is my true calling; it doesn't feel *authentic* to me anymore. I quit this job to become a yoga teacher!" In general, it seems as if "being authentic" frequently relates to saying something negative to someone else in an attempt to modify his or her behavior in some way. *And modifying someone else's behavior does include making that person disappear from one's life.*

It appears that it is difficult to say something authentically positive about someone else. "I authentically love you," doesn't sound quite right — does it? "I authentically believe that your new hairstyle is a wonderful decision!" seems to betray some doubt. One assumption often made about authenticity is that we can be authentic only when decrying our own inauthenticity. This means that an authentic statement can neither be about someone else nor be positive. For example: "I was lacking integrity when I did not return your urgent phone call — I'm really sorry." Or: "I acted passive-aggressively when we were at dinner the other night — please forgive me."

I am not sure we can *only* be authentic when decrying our own inauthenticity, but it is a provocative understanding of authenticity. Try to imagine other ways that we think of authenticity when we hear people use that word. Many times it has to do with vocations and people being trapped in golden handcuffs or life situations they did not foresee. For example: "What I really want to do is paint; but I have two kids in college, and painting will not pay the bills." Or: "I love teaching yoga, but if I quit my corporate job I won't be able to afford the mortgage on my new house."

Vocations are extremely important, and I address them in chapters 5, 7, and 8. For now, let's focus on what we mean when we talk about speaking authentically. The first thing we need to consider is language:

- How does language function?
- How does language relate to thoughts?
- How do thoughts relate to consciousness?
- What thoughts are unconscious?
- Do thoughts exist only in the form of words?
- How do thoughts relate to emotions?
- What are people doing when they speak?

Most of the time we are thinking in particular languages. The majority of my thoughts are in English. Is it possible to have thoughts in our minds that are not in a language? Is it possible to "think" outside of a language? Of course music, painting, sculpture, dancing, and all other art forms, and even making love, are languages. But when we are hungry, we do not normally imagine a sensual Rodin sculpture; we think, "I should get something to eat," and then we go eat something.

Thinking exists within a matrix of culturally accepted assumptions, norms, and mores; feeling exists within a matrix of culturally accepted assumptions, norms, and mores; language exists within a matrix of culturally accepted assumptions, norms, and mores; and writing exists within a matrix of culturally accepted assumptions, norms, and mores. All disciplines, too, such as art, music, politics, economics, and psychology, among others, exist within matrices.

- "Babso dax lanuga dondo" (gibberish) lies outside those agreed-upon assumptions.
- "I feel dead," when not taken as hyperbole meaning "numb," lies outside agreed-upon assumptions about feeling (since dead people, to the best of our knowledge, cannot feel).
- The statement "I am going to eat the neighbor's

puppy for supper" lies outside our agreed-upon
mores.
- "Breathing air is profitable" does not make much
sense.

The fact that a group of people more or less consistently
agree on words meaning or referring to the same or similar concepts and things, constructs what I consider to be a paradigm.
Our society — Western civilization — lies on a bed of agreements buttressed by beliefs that fall under the general categories that we refer to as science, capitalism, and religion. From
our faith in science, capitalism, and religion, we derive our
paradigm of order. Rules and laws dictate and maintain order in
our society. People who disrupt social order are imprisoned or
dispatched. Some of the central assumptions of Western civilization are: property ownership, marriage for life, money, voting,
three meals a day, sex for nonprocreational purposes, inheri-
tances, war, business, banking, debt, fossil fuels, electricity, mass
transportation, media, and, more recently, mobile telephones,
smartphones, the internet, social media, and virtual reality.

Given that the mandate of science is "truth" — which really is a search for an accurate mapping of what's "out there"
(not in our heads) — this leads to a brief but important distinction about truth and subjective/objective duality. Philosopher
Immanuel Kant proposed that objective truth was "out there"
and that we could never know it from our subjective points of
view. I do not believe that truth exists "out there" in the world.
I believe that the people within any paradigm form a consensus regarding what truth (currently) is. They agree on certain
concepts, but upon inspection many of these concepts can be
deconstructed. For example, I could say, "Well, we all agree
that murder is bad," to which you could retort, "What about in

war, or capital punishment — are those not murders?" Philosophers have rhetorically asked: When someone says the word *red*, and another person hears the word *red*, how can we be certain they have mental images of the same color? That does not render the concept of red useless. "Watch out for the rapidly approaching red truck!" is a useful phrase. But certainty on what constitutes red is difficult to achieve, if not impossible, when it is contingent upon language working in conjunction with optical nerves and neurons firing and wiring in our brains. Or definitions may be simply tautological, as in: "Red is red, and it is obvious to everyone — *save the color-blind.*"

The following metaphor is useful regarding the subjective/ objective distinction: "The map is not the territory." Every person has a map in his or her head that maps the reality "out there." However, some people are color-blind, some are tone-deaf, some are myopic; some have wonderful olfactory ranges and taste subtle flavors, and other people do not. In a graduate class in philosophy I attended in 1989, to argue a position, visiting professor Eddy Zemach asked another professor what it was like when that professor's wife experienced an orgasm. (I bet you thought that philosophy couldn't be so much fun!) The professor went into an elaborate and somewhat romantic description of blood surging up from his wife's feet and legs, heat rising and sweat beading, intensification of breathing, moaning, and so on. When he was finished, Professor Zemach disabused him of the notion of being able to know what it was like when his wife had an orgasm: "That's what happens when *you* have an orgasm. You have no idea what it is like for your wife to experience an orgasm. The best you can do is *project* onto her your experience when you have an orgasm."

I cannot see the world from another person's point of view;

I can only see it from my own. The map is not the territory. Or as Magritte demonstrated in his painting *Ceci n'est pas une pipe*, a painting of a pipe is not a pipe. One cannot smoke a painting. Nor can one smoke a word. Language points to phenomena; language indicates. As we will see in my discussions of psychology, it is important to recognize that although we seem to agree on language, every person has a subjective point of view that is based on his or her experiences and the language he or she uses to think about and express those experiences.

But first let's examine how thinking, feeling, and communicating relate to each other: our cultural paradigm recognizes something we call "consciousness" that is a function of our "minds." Although we use the terms *consciousness* and *mind* frequently, if you really think about them they are difficult to define. For example, if I ask you to touch your consciousness or point to your mind, you would probably be flummoxed or at least uncertain. Both consciousness and mind are nonlocal: neither can be reduced to a particular place. Yes, some people point to their heads when asked where their minds reside; others, such as Tibetans, point to their hearts. My point is that many people conflate mind and brain and are quick to speak about neural plasticity and creating neural pathways, about "sensing" in some way their prefrontal cortices and corpus callosums and getting their right hemispheres to interact with their left hemispheres...but it is actually difficult to precisely relate the concepts of mind and brain. *And by* difficult *I mean impossible*. In fact, I prefer to hear a Christian Scientist refuse to go to a hospital for a broken arm because he is convinced that Jesus Christ will heal it, than hear a meditation teacher discuss enlarging his corpus callosum.

What I am asking you to question is the way that the

scientific paradigm has been appropriated by laypeople who really do not understand what has and has not been scientifically proven. Science has made exponential progress over the last few centuries but still does not know how a human brain functions any more than it can explain how gravity causes the tides to move in and out. There are theories. There are *correlations*. Correlations have been observed and noted. But the goal of science is to ascribe *causality*, not correlation. No scientist worth her salt will say, "I have located and isolated the gene that causes people to be homosexual" or "I have mapped particular neurological firings consistent in all human beings that occur when they decide to vote Republican."

Try on this metaphor, please: the brain is the hardware and the mind is the software. Although it is in vogue to discuss neural plasticity and neural pathways, the next time a meditation teacher tells you that you will create new neural pathways when you meditate, please ask him to show you which neural pathways are created. A brain can be discussed only with the aid of a magnetic resonance imaging (MRI) machine. Most people do not have these \$1.5–\$3 million machines constantly at their disposal, so it is easier to reach an agreement about a Jackson Pollock painting than about the electricity bouncing around inside a human head. *Human beings do not have direct introspection into brain states.* At no time in your lifetime will you hear someone say, "Synapses 85,932 and 700,774 just fired. I need to take an aspirin." Or: "I just created a new neural pathway for a color between orange, brown, and green!" You will never hear someone say, "I can feel the dopamine rushing through my brain!" You will hear: "I am happy." You will never hear someone say, "My serotonin levels are very high." You will hear: "I feel good." We must continue to use the concept of mind to mediate between what we sense and feel and how those stimuli are processed through our brain states and then translated into language. We cannot directly see into, or otherwise sense, our brain states or any other parts beneath our skin, so it is inaccurate to talk as if we do. When I speak with neurologists, they tell me they are baffled by the ignorance of laypeople who feel qualified to discuss neural plasticity and how our brains create neural pathways. Of course the brain creates new neural pathways — *so what?* We will never directly observe our brains creating neural pathways, so why is it popular to use these terms today? *Laypeople prefer to have an inaccurate accord about brains than to speak with precision about consciousness.*

In the 1960s, Thomas Kuhn wrote that scientific paradigms shift every generation, or approximately every twenty-five years. He obviously did not anticipate a behemoth such as the internet that would cause paradigm shifts in time periods much shorter than a single generation. Science is a system. And that system is dynamic. If we tried to explain to our grandmothers in 1975 that someday cancer would be manageable, gay people could marry, a black man would be president of the United States, or marijuana would be legal, they would have looked at us askew — the same way you would look at me if I told you that someday marijuana would be mandatory, all religions would be illegal, America would be ruled by a dictator, and the only edible meat left on earth would be from rats. We are all fish swimming in a cultural sea of language and norms and mores that we cannot see, that we consider to be "normal." If in 1950 you had told an American to eat raw fish, he would have laughed in your face, maybe called you a commie pinko. Today there is a sushi restaurant on every other corner. "Normal" changes faster than we imagine.

When exploring what it means to be authentic, we must take cultural context(s), as well as history, into consideration. For example, observe how quickly pathologies shift within one culture: 150 years ago many women were afflicted by something identified as hysteria, during which the patient lost control over her acts and emotions and often fainted or had sudden emotional outbursts and seizures. Hysteria was treated, most notably by Sigmund Freud's teacher Jean-Martin Charcot, with vaginal massages and hysterectomies. Today a vaginal massage by a physician is not a treatment; *it's a lawsuit*. If a woman went into a psychiatrist's office today and listed the above symptoms, the doctor would study the 947-page fifth edition of the *Diagnostic and Statistical Manual of Mental Disorders* (*DSM*) to determine a diagnosis for the ailment and then — since 56 percent of the *DSM*'s authors have been employed at some time by pharmaceutical companies — probably prescribe a medication. Please note that the first two editions of the *DSM*, written before 1973, listed homosexuality as a mental disorder.

If you have the opportunity to spend time with the *DSM* and comb through the fascinating afflictions and disorders that plague people in first-world countries, such as shaky leg syndrome and ADHD (have you met anyone who does not have ADHD?), please ask yourself: "What is the metric of mental well-being in our culture?" The fourth edition of the *DSM* had a "bereavement exemption" for people grieving the loss of a loved one; however, the fifth edition of the *DSM* eliminated the bereavement exemption because psychiatrists found that the same pharmaceuticals used to treat depression were equally effective in treating bereavement. I argue that the barometer of mental health employed in our country is the following: "Are you a productive member of society? Are you able to show up for work? Are you capable of spending most of your waking hours working? Are you able to do your job?" And if you cannot, then there are probably some pills that can inspire you to go back to your lathe, mill, bus, computer, assembly line, orchard, or other work station.

If your best friend told you that she had just spent two weeks lying in bed, eating gummy bears and caramel popcorn, watching reality television, and contemplating the meaning of existence, you would ask, "What's wrong with you?". Maybe something is wrong with her and maybe something is not. Maybe she simply feels as if her limited time visiting planet Earth is more pleasantly spent lying in bed instead of flipping burgers, waiting on tables, or being objectified by men. However, with just a few more symptoms, such as decreased interest or pleasure in most activities, significant weight change (5 percent) or change in appetite, change in sleep, or fatigue, she would be diagnosed as suffering from a major depressive episode and probably offered a prescription for the latest antidepressant medication developed by a multibillion-dollar pharmaceutical company whose sales representatives have wined and dined the doctors while touting the benefits of their products.

Our cultural context is sometimes identified by the acronym WEIRD: Western, educated, industrialized, rich, democratic. But WEIRD populations represent only a fraction of the world. This means that a ten-year-old boy in Papua New Guinea anxiously searching for coconuts so that his family can eat that day probably should not be given a diagnosis of ADHD. Things considered problematic in one culture are not ubiquitous throughout the world. And if the boy in Papua New

Guinea fails to find those coconuts, he probably should not be diagnosed with depression either.

Most of us trust doctors with our physical health — *and rightly so*. But did you know that until 150 years ago, surgery was performed in barbershops and the anesthesia was whiskey? If you are aware of the progress made in stem cell research, then you will agree that the barbaric and torturous procedure known as a root canal treatment is, thankfully, headed toward the dustbin of history. What about our mental health? What about our emotional lives? Should we not question how and why diagnoses come and go? If you went to a doctor today and she diagnosed you with hysteria, what would you think? Why don't you have the same reaction when she diagnoses you with depression and anxiety? My point is that the scientific ground beneath our feet is elastic: the paradigm of what constitutes mental and emotional well-being is contingent upon myriad factors, including the very definitions of diseases, disorders, addictions, and afflictions and their origins — which are being perpetually revised and amended. If you ever received a diagnosis, how did you fit it into your personal identity?

The influence of the medical and pharmaceutical industries should not be underestimated when discussing authenticity. At some point in time, most people have been diagnosed with a medical issue; afterward, they had to decide whether to wear it like Hester Prynne's scarlet letter or use it as an excuse for some behavior, attack it, deny it, or ignore it. The model for what constitutes well-being in our society only exists negationally: it is defined by what it is not. If you look closely at the information about nutrition you received while growing up — the four food groups, three meals a day, how your body runs, how to fix parts that break down, and so on — you might start to question why so many people take pharmaceuticals on a daily basis and how these chemicals and our understanding of our diseases and disorders shape our consciousness.

In particular, there has been an increase of people in our culture — particularly younger people — diagnosed with depression and anxiety. We will examine the relationship between our minds' negativity biases and depression and anxiety throughout the rest of this book, but for now let's focus on the thoughts that continually race around our minds. It is commonly agreed that most Americans have thousands of thoughts during the waking hours of each day — most of which are the same as yesterday's thoughts and most of which are negative. For the sake of argument, let's agree that thoughts appear in our minds as words. Because the English language now contains over 1 million words, it often feels as if thinking is infinite, boundless, as if we can think anything, everything — doesn't it? Other times thoughts race so quickly that it seems almost impossible to maintain focus on unified threads for more than a few minutes at a time. And this bombardment is usually continuous until we drift off to sleep or figure out some way to get into a "zone" of clarity, such as by running or swimming or practicing yoga; conversely, we can also distract ourselves with alcohol, tobacco, narcotics, overeating, pharmaceuticals, video games, television, pornography, shopping, or other diversions.

If we analyze the thoughts and behavior of most people, and realize that the vast majority of thoughts that spring to consciousness are not original and also not necessary for our survival, we could equally assert that language is a cage. In *The Gay Science*, Nietzsche writes, "The whole of life would be possible without its seeing itself as it were in a mirror: as in fact even at present the far greater part of our life still goes

on without this mirroring, and even our thinking, feeling, voli-
tional life as well, however painful this statement may sound to
an older philosopher. What then is the purpose of consciousness
generally, when it is in the main superfluous?" Nietzsche even
provocatively poses the possibility that only the worst and most
superficial thoughts are the ones that rise to consciousness.

*How is it that this immense gift — consciousness — that
distinguishes us from most other animals could be so inefficient?*
Dolphins have not traveled to the moon yet. Orangutans did
not build computers. Alligators have not created steady food
supply systems yet. How could human consciousness with all
of its astonishing creations have become so detrimental to so
many people in such a short period of time? Including war
deaths, over one hundred million murders were committed in
the twentieth century. According to the American Foundation
for Suicide Prevention, there are 121 suicides in America every
day. Do any other species compare in their malevolence? In
their self-hatred? In depression? Most wild animals cannot
afford the luxury of being depressed, since that would make
them more susceptible to being caught and eaten by predators. Human consciousness appears to be both a blessing and a
curse.

If we are trapped within the languages that we speak, and
trapped within the cultural contexts in which we grew up and
live, *then what could possibly constitute authenticity?* When we
meditate and taste the nectar of bliss beyond language, is that
the authentic self? The Higher Self? The self without worries
and anxiety and fear? If you practice Transcendental Meditation, then it would be the Higher Self. If you are sitting to meditate, in the Hindu lineage, and you repeat in your mind the
words "I am meditating, I am meditating, I am meditating..."

then you are not meditating. In that tradition, to meditate means to transcend maya, everything you perceive through your five senses that is chunked into narratives and judged by your mind. The result of Transcendental Meditation — that state of transcending your senses and your mind — is paralinguistic. You can be consciously aware of it only retrospectively. Conversely, the Buddhist-derived set of mindfulness meditations helps train the mind and prevent it from dragging us around the way wild horses would. When teaching any meditation in which students observe their own thoughts, I ask them afterward to "please point to the part of you that was observing your thoughts." As previously stated, most people point to their heads. But philosophers and scientists agree that the mind is nonlocal. How and why do we have this capacity to monitor the phrases that arise in our consciousness? Where does that exist? Is the mind akin to, or analogous to, the operating system software that runs your computer? If it is, then meditation functions like rebooting the hard drive, emptying the cache, and starting afresh. Which is why people practice it daily.

In the Hindu tradition of Vedanta, discussed in chapter 7, yoga and meditation were designed to help us transcend our minds so that we could realize our authentic selves. According to the Upanishads, what we find through meditation and yoga is that the Atman — our Higher Self or our soul — is really at one with Brahman, that our true essence is actually at one with literally everything, and that separation is illusory. It is the daily functioning of our minds — the thousands of redundant and mostly negative thoughts — that obfuscates the fact that we are essentially divine, whole, and interconnected with everyone and everything.

More on the benefits of meditation later. For now, let's

examine why most of our thoughts are redundant and negative, and what our culture regards psychologically as our "authentic selves." To paraphrase psychologist D. W. Winnicott, children develop "false selves" — facades, personas — in order to survive and try to get their emotional and psychological needs meet. I would argue that in Western civilization, most of children's interactions with adults entail some form of behavior modification, with rewards and punishments. We could even say that we tame children in much the same way that we tame pets in our culture. Children want to sleep when they are tired, eat when they are hungry, defecate when they need to defecate, and play when they feel playful. But fairly soon after birth we put them on schedules with designated feeding times, sleep times, and play times; when they get to school there are even designated bathroom breaks. But that is not the bad part; the bad part is that we primarily train them to be productive members of society through negative languaging: "*Don't* stick your tongue into the socket." "*Don't* eat with your hands." "*Don't* wake Mommy before six o'clock." "*Don't* run out into traffic." "*Don't* poop in your diapers anymore." "*Don't* get bad grades." "*Don't* do drugs." "*Don't* play with your genitals." "*Don't...don't...don't...*"

And then we wonder why there is an epidemic of "negative self-talk" and "low self-esteem" in our culture. Was any child born with a voice in her head that said, "I stink. I am no good at anything"? Or as Hamlet says, "I could accuse me of such things that it were better my mother had not borne me."

To make matters even worse, children assimilate anything that seems awry in their worlds by telling themselves: "There must be something wrong with me," as in: "Mommy would not have a migraine if I were a good girl" or "My parents would not have gotten divorced if I were a good boy." Children fall into line and develop false selves to avoid negative feedback from the authority figures in their lives and to gain acceptance, approval, and love from everyone with whom they interact. They learn that they are liked more when they smile. They learn that crying and screaming often disturb other people in their proximity. As a result, sometimes our facades are incongruent with what we are really feeling. We all have a way of being in the world — the way we stand, the way we speak, the way we smile, the way we look concerned, the way we dress, the way we focus our eyes, the way we furrow our brows, the way we wring our hands, the way we wear our shoulders, the way we brag or are self-deprecating, the way we portray ourselves as heroes or victims, the way we think about mortality or do not, the subjects we discuss... All of these things we develop as we individuate from our caregivers and become independent. Maybe sarcasm helped you survive your adolescence by diffusing tense situations or making people like you because you were humorous? Maybe crying made people feel sorry for you and forced them to stop criticizing you? People usually have very little insight into their own way of being.

As sentient beings, we wish to be loved *unconditionally* — that is what I believe our "authentic selves" seek. But fairly early in life, we learn that most "love" or positive feedback that we receive is contingent upon our behavior. Being quiet and smiling gets us rewarded with smiles and pats on the head. Screaming or emotional outbursts get us punished, sent to our rooms, and maybe even get our iPads taken away. Egads! If we act in ways that displease our caregivers, then we are punished until we act in ways that please them. So we create false selves, or facades, in order to gain acceptance, to seduce people into liking us — because we are smart or talented or pretty or well-behaved or refined or accomplish certain things. However, this dynamic ultimately functions as a giant resentment factory, because we are constantly seducing people into liking or loving our outer selves, and then we eventually resent them for not loving our authentic selves, *the "authentic selves" that we have never, or seldom, shown them.* Obviously our authentic selves (psychologically) are too unseemly for public display. In fact, our culture recognizes only a narrow bandwidth of acceptable emotions: we dislike angry women and we dislike sad men. Grieving the loss of his father, Hamlet is told by Claudius: "'Tis unmanly grief. It shows a will most incorrect to heaven, / A heart unfortified, a mind impatient, / An understanding simple and unschooled."

As previously stated, I believe that the tacit barometer for mental order in our culture is working, showing up for our jobs, and being productive. And if we are too sad or angry to work, then we must be truly unwell. But maybe our authentic selves are angry or sad for having to create false selves to seduce people into liking us? Maybe we get tired of jumping through hoops for other people? Is it possible that what we call "midlife crises" occur when there is a crack in consciousness and people realize that if they did not have such a glitzy facade, their family members and fair-weather friends would stop returning their text messages and phone calls? Nobody wants a spouse who is with him because he can afford expensive cars and vacations; and yet so many online dating profiles show people standing in front of their expensive cars or on expensive vacations. A conundrum.

Every time we are forced, as children, to jump through hoops in order to get love or positive feedback, this foments resentment. And even if there was no physical trauma during our childhoods, all of these resentments can add up to what is often called "a core wound." As adults, we have remnants of wounded children in us. These wounded children still imitate the traits of the adults we loved as children, and they do so in order to subconsciously gain acceptance, approval, and love from those we thought withheld acceptance, approval, and love from us; but we also rebelled and reacted against those same authorities as a way of individuating, or becoming our own selves. As a consequence, we experience tension resulting from the confluence of reinforcements we received from adults and peers while being raised in a highly competitive society. In short, we emulate the characteristics of the caregivers we had when we were young in an attempt to retroactively sub-consciously gain their approval and love; and we also subcon-sciously incarnate the opposite characteristics of the caregivers we had when we were young as a way of individuating from them. Becoming something in order to gain approval is inau-thentic; being reactive and rebelling against something is also inauthentic. How can we know what is authentic if there are wounded children in all of us seeking the approval of and indi-viduating from people who may not even be a part of our lives anymore?

So if *authentic*, in its colloquial meaning, is really a justifi-cation for saying something negative to someone else, and the cultural meaning of *authentic* seems like an excuse to quit a job you hate and become a yoga teacher or life coach (or both), and the spiritual and philosophical meanings of the term are too esoteric and airy-fairy, and the psychological meanings make it seem impossible... *then what is authenticity and how can we be authentic?*

Maybe authenticity relates to being congruent, when our outsides match our insides, our intentions? Maybe authenticity really just means being present and as little prejudiced as possible within the confines of a culture and a language? Maybe it relates to our way of being in the world? I address all these questions in later chapters. But before we attempt to be authentic, we must examine how we became inauthentic.

Chapter 2

How to Avoid Being a Professional Child

I n the beginning was the word.

But not in our beginnings.

Our beginnings were rather heated soupy affairs with probably more primordial screams and cries than actual words used by us or our mothers. Through our mothers' umbilical cords we received sustenance until we were ejected from their wombs, the cords were cut, and we were held in someone's arms. Somehow we instinctually sensed that we were helpless. Totally helpless. Completely dependent on people, much larger people, to make sure that nipples — human or artificial — found their way to the vicinity of our mouths, that our bottoms were cleaned when they became messy, and that we were provided with safe, comfortable places to sleep.

We cried a lot. Words came much later.

In the 1930s, French psychiatrist Jacques Lacan developed what would become his essay "Le stade du miroir," or "The Mirror Phase." Lacan theorized that when a baby is initially held up to a mirror, it cannot see "itself," its "self" — cannot recognize its own hands, head, eyes, nose, mouth, legs, and so on — because it has no "self," no individual identity (yet).

A baby cannot conceive of itself as an entity separate from its mother or other caregivers. It does not recognize a reflection of its own beingness. Then, as the baby develops, it spies some things in a mirror and recognizes them as its own hands, head, eyes, nose, mouth, legs, and so on. In this way, its "self," knowledge of its own beingness and distinct separateness from its mother and/or caregivers, as well as its subjective experience of everything outside of it, are born. This is known as the individuation process. But as I will later argue, there are several types of individuation processes in our culture, so I refer to this initial self-recognition as the first individuation process, when the baby gains its sense of self apart from its mother and/or other primary caregivers.

In terms of twentieth-century psychology, this is when our individual egos are born. For the purposes of this book I introduce the following analogy to distinguish between the terms *ego* and *mind*: the mind is like a junior high school classroom, and the ego is like the teacher. The teacher organizes, directs, and governs all of the often unruly students (thoughts). There are sundry nuanced definitions of ego by psychiatrists such as Sigmund Freud and Carl Jung that do not directly pertain to attachment theory, so I do not address them here.

In our culture, *ego* often refers to esteem, and there appears to be a range of healthy and unhealthy degrees of ego/esteem that one can have. In the colloquial understanding of *ego*, the phrase "He has low self-esteem" implies that the person's ego has been battered by unruly negative thoughts; in the other extreme, "He's a narcissist" means that his ego is too strong, selfish, impervious, and rigid. To call someone selfish in French, you would say, "Elle est égoïste." Again, let's think of the ego as the governing or regulating mechanism of the mind. The ego is born when the child can recognize itself as separate from its mother and/or caregivers; the ego develops throughout the individuation process(es) as the child gains independence and masters certain skills. I am not certain that we can easily define what a "healthy" or "normal" ego would be; usually I speak in terms of patients' abilities to regulate their emotional reactions, but that process is slightly more physical than mental (i.e., patients' abilities to manage their anger and use tools to deal with sadness, frustration, disappointment, loneliness). However, we all recognize when someone has an unhealthy ego — one that is either too weak or too strong. The main point is that the ego, or teacher, in the classroom of the mind is not unaffected by his students, his thoughts. Although he is tasked with governing the students, sometimes they become so transgressive that the ego has a meltdown and is overrun, overwhelmed, and rendered useless.

As we begin to individuate and become more and more independent, we develop attachment styles. Some infants do their best to please their caregivers; others are more rebellious (e.g., "the terrible twos," when infants seemingly bathe in the pleasure of uttering the word *no*). The following questions will help us understand how attachment styles that may have developed in infancy affect our subconscious assumptions about the world "out there" and how those assumptions influence our adult relationships:

- As adults are we, in general, trusting or suspicious of other people?
- Do we feel that the world is an inherently safe or dangerous place?
- Do we feel that there is an abundance of resources, or that resources are scarce?

- Is it possible that our general understanding regarding safety and our ability to trust other people were developed even before we could speak and still affect us today now that we are adults?

- Do we assume that other people are naturally generous and concerned about our well-being?

- Do we have default voices in our heads that say, "If I turn my back on someone, he will hurt me or take advantage of, betray, or violate me"?

- How do we feel when a family member asks to borrow ten thousand dollars? What about when a friend asks to borrow ten thousand dollars? An acquaintance? A stranger?

- How many people can we depend on? How many people "have our backs" right now? If one hour from now we found ourselves in a hospital or jail, how many people would accept our phone calls, drop what they are doing, and come help us?

- And conversely, how many people can rely on us? How many people would say, "Ira has my back," right now? If one hour from now one of these people found himself in a hospital or jail, would we accept his phone call, drop whatever we are doing, and go help him?

In the late 1950s, British psychiatrist John Bowlby developed what is known today as attachment theory. He noticed that babies became distressed when their mothers were absent. *Go figure.* Bowlby believed that children's relationships with their mothers shaped their social, emotional, and cognitive development, and that there were links between how babies attached to their mothers and how those babies grew up to be either well-adjusted or maladjusted adults.

In the 1960s, Mary Ainsworth conducted experiments known as "the Strange Situation" to test how securely babies were attached to their mothers, to observe the babies' reactions and responses to being left alone, and then to see how they re-attached to their mothers. (If you are interested, you can find many videos of the Strange Situation or experiments replicating it on the internet.) Ainsworth's experiment was set up in a small room with a one-way mirror so that the infants' behaviors could be observed covertly. Babies were between twelve and eighteen months old, and she tested around a hundred middle-class American families. The experiment consisted of eight episodes lasting approximately three minutes each. Here is the protocol for the eight sections:

1. The mother, baby, and experimenter are in a room, and then the experimenter leaves.
2. The mother and baby are alone in the room.
3. A stranger joins the mother and infant.
4. The mother leaves the baby and stranger alone.
5. The mother returns and the stranger leaves.
6. The mother leaves and the infant is left completely alone.
7. The stranger comes back into the room.
8. The mother returns and the stranger leaves.

Ainsworth was looking for four things:

- Does the baby experience separation anxiety and distress when the mother leaves her with the stranger?
- Does the baby avoid the stranger when alone with

her but become friendly with the stranger when the
mother is present?

- How does the baby reunite with the mother when
  she returns? Is the baby positive and happy when
  the mother returns? Does the child resist and possibly even push the mother away? Does the child
  seem disinterested?
- Does the baby use the mother as a safe base from
  which to explore their environment? Can the mother
  and stranger comfort the infant equally well?

From her observations, Ainsworth deduced that babies' attachment styles could be grouped into three main categories:

- Secure attachment
- Ambivalent attachment
- Avoidant attachment

Later, a fourth category was added called disorganized attachment.

Secure attachment occurs when parents are emotionally
available, perceptive, responsive, and attuned to babies' physical and emotional needs. Babies whose parents enabled this
style of attaching are secure in their sense of self and in trusting
others to respond in a safe, nurturing, and fair manner. They
are able to ask for assistance when needed. Babies with secure
attachment styles remained relatively calm, seeming to be secure in the belief that their caregivers would not put them in
harm's way and would return shortly.

In contrast, babies who did not have secure attachment styles
would cry and become distressed, even possibly distraught.
Among those children who became distressed, three types of in-
secure attachment were denoted:

Ambivalent: Parents were inconsistently available, perceptive, and responsive, but also somewhat intrusive. Babies who had this attachment style present as anxious and demanding of others, needing constant reassurance and looking to others for their self-esteem and worth.

Avoidant: Parents were emotionally unavailable, imperceptive, unresponsive and did not attune to the babies' emotions and needs. Babies with this style are fearful of rejection and avoid intimacy and attachment with others. While babies may grow up to appear self-sufficient and independent, this usually masks a deep fear of rejection/abandonment.

Disorganized: Parents were frightening, alarming, emotionally dysregulated, and often showed disapproval and anger. The behavior of babies with this style is often chaotic and confusing; in adults this would manifest as being hot and cold in relationships, pulling others toward them then inexplicably pushing them away.

Even before we learn to speak, it appears, we develop attachment styles or ways of connecting to others — secure, ambivalent, avoidant, or disorganized — that represent our perceptions and conceptions of our own safety, well-being, and how much we can trust and depend on other people. In relation to the questions raised in chapter 1 regarding authenticity, what would it mean to be authentic if we have styles of attaching and interacting with other people, and/or trust or safety or independence issues, that we developed even before we could speak?

As a psychotherapist who has spent his entire adult life in urban environments such as Paris, Los Angeles, Manhattan, Philadelphia, Austin, Santa Barbara, and Berkeley, I realize that I interact with a skewed population sample, but I do not think that the majority of adults I have met exhibit the characteristics representative of secure attachment. What is your experience of other people? Do you meet many who are relatively steady, stable, and dependable, who can maintain committed careers and relationships such as marriage for life or serial monogamy, plus solid long-lasting friendships, with little drama, few complaints, and no underlying dissatisfaction? Seeing as the divorce rate in America is 40 percent, I think we can make the argument that our attachment muscles are not as strong as they were during the thousands of years that humans lived in tribes of about 150 extended-family members.

For eons, babies and small children rarely left their mothers' arms — they slept with their mothers or parents and breast-fed until age four or five. *You realize that human beings are the only mammals that drink the breast milk of another mammal, and that it is a sign of economic success in our society that babies do not sleep in the same beds as their parents — right?* In third-world countries, babies spend much more of their time in their early years physically attached to their mothers. In many first-world countries, mothers return to work and babies are fed and taken care of by day-care nurseries, nannies, and schools even before they are toilet trained.

For the sake of argument let's assume that being brought up in a highly competitive, capitalistic first-world country unintentionally accelerates the individuation process. However, let's entertain the possibility that the psychological situation could actually be much more dire than I am conveying: according to the founder of primal therapy, Arthur Janov, when a baby is put down alone for the first time — say, in its own room while the parents sleep in another room — and allowed to "cry itself out" (cry until it is so exhausted that its only option is to fall asleep), the baby registers being put down as: *"Why are you leaving me alone to die? You are killing me!"* (Yes, I am intentionally making a pun: "put down" means "lay to sleep" with infants but "euthanize" with pets.) Janov argues that being put down for the first time creates a core, or primal, betrayal/ abandonment wound in many people. Later in life, according to this theory, when our partner cheats on us or we are fired from a job we love, we become distraught because this betrayal/ abandonment reopens our core betrayal/abandonment wound. Babies simply want to be loved and taken care of; when they feel abandoned, they sense their own dependence on others and their own lack of autonomy, and they tend to freak out.

Like psychoanalysis or Reichian therapy or Jungian therapy or cognitive behavioral therapy, primal therapy is obviously just one theory or model, and it is currently scientifically un- provable using MRI machines or any other electronic devices. But do you know people who become seemingly irrationally dysregulated when they feel abandoned or betrayed? Have you ever met a heartbroken lovelorn teenager carrying around a dog-eared copy of *Romeo and Juliet?* It would be interesting to compare the reactions to divorce of adults who both breast-fed and slept with their mothers until age four or five to the reac- tions of adults who as babies were breast-fed for one year (or not at all) and learned to sleep alone after a few months.

It is difficult to imagine that, during the individuation pro- cess, when we are gaining our individual sense of self, the way our caregivers interact with us does not shape us and possibly affect the relationships we will have as adults, as proposed by John Bowlby. For example, if we are the kind of person who attaches securely to others, and someone does not respond to a text or email we sent, we do not think much of it; however, if we attach insecurely to people and a partner does not respond to a message when we think they are free and should respond to it, then we may become suspicious and make assumptions about the person and relationship that may not correspond to reality. When your partner does not answer a text at lunchtime, do you think, "Oh, he must be busy," or does your mind jump to: "Maybe he is having an affair"?

Do you recognize any of your own patterns, or the way you were individuated, in these descriptions of attachment styles? Have you had, or have you ever witnessed in a partner or friend, what is now called "codependent" behavior? Have any of your friends ever told you that they hacked into their spouse's email account to see if he or she was having an affair? Suspicion, mistrust, and obsessive jealousy are signs of codependent behavior. If you look on the internet for a local Alcoholics Anonymous meeting, you will probably find that the same venue hosts CoDA (Co-Dependents Anonymous) meetings at alternative times. For more information on codependent behavior, please read Melody Beattie's *Codependent No More* and Pia Mellody's *Facing Love Addiction*.

When we become conscious of our primary attachment style, we can make healthy, or healthier, decisions when our guts tell us to "lean in" or to avoid something — whether to trust someone or to flee before we get hurt. Being authentic means not allowing the fear-based prejudices that we subconsciously learned as children to rule our adult lives. Let's look at the mind's negativity biases and how and why many people feel stressed and in fight-or-flight mode for many of their waking hours.

I believe that the primary goals of consciousness are to keep us alive and to stave off trauma or potential future trauma.

Now if I am correct (and I may not be), then self-harm or the extreme of self-harm — self-annihilation — would be extremely difficult. Consider the statistics: each year, for every successful suicide in America (around forty thousand), there are twenty-five failures. The human body is astonishingly resilient. Most people misjudge how many pills they need to take, how long the rope should be, where they need to shoot or cut, from how high they need to jump, and so on. Our survival instincts are extremely strong. We are hardwired to avert pain, and death is often preceded by pain. I address suicidal ideation later, but for now let's figure out how and why a human being could develop such an extreme form of "negative self-talk" that his or her inner monologue convinces him or her to attempt suicide.

If you have ever had the privilege of going to a rehab facility or twelve-step meeting, then you would think there is an epidemic of negative self-talk, of low self-esteem — of voices saying, "Not good enough" or "I will be happy in the future when I..." in the heads of people in Western society. How did those critical voices get there? As I noted earlier, I believe we raise children and form them into productive members of society in much the same way that we tame pets: with rewards and punishments. Children want to sleep when they are tired, eat when they are hungry, defecate when they need to defecate, and play when they feel playful. But fairly soon after they are born, we put babies on schedules: there are designated feeding times, sleep times, and play times; when they get to school there are designated bathroom breaks. And much of the taming comes in the form of negative feedback — frowns, negative languaging, *love withheld in some manner* — until the babies realize that something is wrong and that they must act another way in order to receive the sustenance they depend on to survive and the love they crave. However, according to most developmental psychologists, infants do not think, "There is something wrong with the situation — I must change my behavior." Instead, infants think, "There is something wrong with *me*."

When adult patients in my office make generalizations such as "I suck, I am bad at everything, nothing I do goes right, nobody likes me...," I ask them: "Whose voice is that? Were you born with that voice? Were you born thinking that you cannot do anything right? Or by chance did you have critical parents, siblings, teachers, or caretakers?"

Many of us have inner critical voices that appear soon after we accomplish anything. On a grand scale this is also known as a "hedonic treadmill," where the mind replaces desires with fresh desires soon after each is achieved. This "you're not good enough" voice tells us, "Yes, it is great that I made vice president, but I will be happy only when I become president," or "I will be happy when...my net worth is north of $10 million, I marry the perfect spouse, my kids graduate college, my paintings hang in museums, my band plays in a stadium, my internet company goes public, I win the lottery, I have sex twice a day, once a day, once a week...*ever again*."

Anyone who says "I will be happy when I..." will never be happy. Or, more precisely, there will be intermittent feelings of accomplishment quickly followed by new goals to accomplish. Ironically, one of the inalienable rights of Americans is the right to pursue happiness. *Pursuing happiness is a surefire way to misery.* I discuss this more in chapter 8, when I explore the second noble truth of Buddhism, but here are my favorite quotes that convey the paradoxes of happiness:

Happiness cannot be pursued. You do not find happiness; happiness finds you. It is not an end in itself, but a by-product of other activities, often arriving when it is least expected.

— MICK BROWN

There are two tragedies in life. One is not to get your heart's desire. The other is to get it.

— GEORGE BERNARD SHAW

America is among the richest countries in the world, and in 2016 it was ranked as the thirteenth-happiest in the world, behind Denmark, Switzerland, Iceland, Norway, Finland, Canada, Netherlands, New Zealand, Australia, Sweden, Israel, and Austria. How is it possible that we are some of the most privileged human beings to ever walk the face of the earth and not the happiest? According to Ken Dychtwald most human beings who ever lived never reached the age of forty (currently our life expectancy is almost double that); according to the World Bank, 767 million of our fellow human beings lived on less than $1.90 a day in 2013; yet over 20 million Americans take antidepressants daily.

There is an old Freudian slip/joke that says, "Well, if it's not one thing, it's your mother!" I am not blaming post–World War II parenting styles for a few generations of depressed people; I am asking you to look at the Western paradigm buttressed by capitalism, science, and religion and consider whether there are unintended psychological and emotional ramifications to the way children are raised in our society. Parenting is the toughest job in the world. There is no such creature as the perfect parent. It is a balancing act. It is a dance. And we are fortunate that there are so many wonderful resources to help parents today, such as Shefali Tsabary's book *The Conscious Parent* and *Mindful Parenting* by Kristen Race.

Einstein said that the level of consciousness that created a problem will be unable to fix it. So it is time to start examining how the way we raise children correlates with the rise of mental disorders such as depression, ADHD, general anxiety disorder, and so on.

- Are our schools too competitive and stressful?
- Are sports and games too competitive and stressful?
- Is "fitting in" — being accepted by others and having friends — unduly competitive and stressful?
- Do media such as video games, Instagram, Twitter, Snapchat, texting, movies, television, popular music, romance novels, and magazines, as well as the apparent worship of celebrities, help to raise stable, well-adjusted children?

You may be familiar with what has come to be known as the "marshmallow test." It was a study conducted by psychologist Walter Mischel at Stanford University in 1960. Children four to six years of age were offered a treat such as a marshmallow, cookie, or pretzel and told that if they waited fifteen minutes without eating the treat they would receive a second treat. Videos of various incarnations of this experiment available online showing the children as they try to resist the treats confronting them are hysterical, disturbing, and bizarre — with some children covering their eyes to hide the treats from themselves and one girl going so far as to bang her head against the desk in an attempt to thwart temptation and muster discipline.

One-third of the children were able to resist enjoying instant gratification. But that is not the interesting part of the experiment; what is interesting is that twenty and thirty years later, researchers found that the children who were able to delay gratification had done better in school, had better careers and better relationships, and were more successful overall. *If parents want to raise successful children, and they know that self-discipline is essential to success, then how do they instill that quality while avoiding inadvertently informing the children that there is something wrong with them?* Again, it is a balancing act, a dance. And luckily there are books such as *Mindful Discipline: A Loving Approach to Setting Limits and Raising an Emotionally Intelligent Child* by Shauna Shapiro and Chris White to help parents today.

I am not suggesting that we blame our parents for our failed relationships as adults. Instead I am trying to provoke you to ask the question "If many of my redundant and negative thoughts can be traced back to my childhood, then what is my authentic self?" Myriad factors contribute to how our minds develop as we grow up, but why is it that people in WEIRD populations are plagued with redundant and negative thoughts? Obviously this epidemic of negative self-talk, which psychotherapists can attest to, is inauthentic. No understanding of authenticity would include such horrifying low self-esteem or its converse — narcissism — which, I argue, is often just a mask for low self-esteem.

Aside from our attachment styles, and depending on our individual paradigms, there may also be even more esoteric factors that are not scientifically provable and that influence who we are and how we think, such as karma, astrology, meridians, chakras, kundalini energy, doshas, koshas, birth order, how and what we were fed, where and how much we slept, and the infinite interactions we had with others before we could think or speak. The important question to ask when we notice negative voices that we obviously were not born with is: "Whose voice is that telling me I am not good enough? Whose voice is telling me I will be happy or happier if/when I accomplish X in the future?"

The reason we should be cognizant of the dynamics we have with each of our parents is because these probably manifest as attachment styles. For example, if our fathers or mothers were aloof and emotionally withholding, we should not be surprised if we are attracted to partners who turn out to be aloof and withholding; if our fathers or mothers were smothering and coddling, we should not be surprised if we are attracted to partners who turn out to be smothering and coddling. Also, we rebel in order to individuate and declare ourselves as autonomous agents, and so we should not be surprised if we are also attracted to the exact opposites of our parents: if our fathers or mothers were aloof and emotionally withholding, we may subconsciously seek out partners who are smothering and coddling; if our fathers or mothers were smothering and coddling, we may subconsciously seek out partners who are aloof and withholding. There is tension because we emulate the characteristics of the caregivers we had when we were young as a way of trying to retroactively subconsciously gain their approval and love; we also subconsciously incarnate their opposite characteristics as a way of individuating from them. Becoming something or someone to gain approval is inauthentic; being reactive and rebelling against something is also inauthentic.

Specifically, the wounded child in each of us feels betrayed because all he or she wanted was to be loved *unconditionally* and grew up in a society that primarily provided tools to gain love *conditionally* — because we behaved correctly, learned to use forks and toilets (not at the same time), received good grades in school, looked good, were good athletes, spoke well, earned money, were fashionable or had "good taste," and so on. This creates much resentment because, even as children, we felt as if we were constantly "seducing" people into liking our outer selves, our false selves, facades, and personas. However, the tools we learned to use to seduce people in this way are often not the right tools for procuring the type of love our hearts yearn for later in life — they are more apt for procuring admiration. Let me ask: Would we rather be admired or loved?

In an effort to individuate, we sometimes date and marry people who are the exact opposite of one of our parents. Rebellion is an essential part of the individuation processes, but it can also be inauthentic if it means merely moving away from something, rather than also moving toward something. As I see it, people individuate the first time when, as babies, they recognize their reflection in a mirror (as something distinct from their mothers); then again when they go to preschool or school for the first time while still living in their parents' homes; then again if they go to college away from home but are still financially supported by their parents; and then again when they live away from their parents and learn how to independently support themselves as adults. There is tension between having to obey and depend on parents and wanting to be autonomous agents. Note the spate of young people in the last thirty-five to forty years who tattooed their bodies early in life; I see this is a subconscious declaration: "This is my body, and nobody can tell me what to do or what not to do with it anymore (even if you are still paying my rent)!"

In addition, we are living in fascinatingly complex and often confusing times regarding gender roles, the ways we expect men and women to act. We all agree that women should be paid salaries equal to those of men, yet many people still think men should pay for meals, a gesture in which they symbolically enact the role of provider and protector. For some adults there is even tension between wanting to be independent and wanting to be taken care of or demonstratively cared for. We live in a society that has objectified women as sexy secretaries, waitresses, librarians, bank tellers, store clerks, nurses, and so on. That archetype of the damsel in distress, who needs to be "saved" or taken care of is — thankfully! — dying. Women are becoming more and more empowered. But how do we move into the next paradigm of compassion, respect, equality, and love?

One way is through conscious loving and authentic communications. This is when we are mindfully aware of our wounds and how we learned to compensate for them as children. Usually there is some level of inauthenticity regarding the "assets," or false selves, we developed to get our emotional and psychological needs met as children. We must be aware of how we learned to seduce people into liking our false selves, facades, and personas and be brave enough to be authentic and vulnerable (which can be scary). And the first thing we need is loving, nonjudgmental relationships with people who are empathetic and who accept us wholly, not just the glitzy exterior that we were taught to show the world — in particular, the way most of us choose to present our lives through social media rarely gives a balanced, authentic portrayal of our lives.

Ram Dass said, "If you think you're enlightened go spend a week with your family." Although Americans enjoy more privileges and freedoms than people in many other countries, we grow up in a highly competitive society, where children are constantly pushed to get good grades and "achieve" various goals daily, weekly, monthly, and yearly. Whoever pushed us — usually our family members — wounded us by subconsciously informing us that whatever we did was "not good enough." Even positive statements like "You'll do better next time" may have unintentionally informed us that we were failures in some way. In adulthood, all of that (totally unintentional) wounding during childhood adds up to low self-worth, low self-esteem, and feeling unlovable or only conditionally lovable because we "do" certain things or look a certain way or have attained certain goals or a certain status.

Ram Dass's famous quote becomes particularly poignant later in life whenever we actually do visit our primary caretakers, because that is often when we get triggered and our childhood wounds, or core wounds, are reopened. If I receive emergency phone calls from patients during the holiday season, I usually end up telling them: "That fight you are having with your mother/father/sister/brother is not about what you think it is about." And then we discuss things that happened during the patient's childhood — abandonments, betrayals, violations, humiliations, frustrations, feeling unheard, resentment for being told what to do and who to be, and so on — and we figure out what is going on at a subconscious level and at least develop a more interesting narrative.

The best tool I have found for these situations is mindfulness, because it teaches us to cultivate *nonreactivity*. Not reacting to dynamics that were established twenty, thirty, forty, or fifty years ago is definitely the best way to modify them. And then we can make healthier, more compassionate long-term decisions that bode favorably for peace, love, and harmony.

The next time you are with family members and the

situation gets heated, try thinking phrases to yourself such as: "Wow...isn't that interesting! All of my daddy abandonment/withholding [whatever your core issue is] buttons are being pushed right now! I thought I had resolved that issue a long time ago! This is so interesting!" And then you can decide to take a walk or do something healthy instead of reacting and exacerbating the situation.

In particular, all "observing thoughts meditations" can be helpful. Please visit YouTube and spend a few minutes doing such meditations every day. You can think of it as exercising a muscle, as going to a gym for your mind. Once we learn to sit and observe how our minds operate, then when we are in situations that trigger us, we can make healthy choices — like choosing just to observe the triggers and being proud of ourselves for not reacting. For example, let's say we are visiting our parents and our father or mother asks us to drive him or her to the store. Everything is going swimmingly until we have to park and our parent starts looking around nervously, then tells us: "More to the left, no now to the right — I said more to the left...no, more to the right." He or she is trying to help us parallel park, but the wounded child in us hears: "I can never do anything right." Mindfulness helps us direct our attention to the present moment, be in the present moment, and ignore and dissipate the negative voices that stem from our childhood.

In summary, we have examined potential unintended subconscious ramifications of growing up in Western culture, and how being molded into a productive member of society might have affected our mental health and relationships as an adult.

Here are three questions I would like you to remember as we move forward:

1. If our minds are not born with negative self-talk, then where does it come from?

2. Is it possible that depression and many other mood disorders are culturally contingent, that they are reactions to being continuously forced to jump through hoops for crumbs of the unconditional love that we crave?

3. As a society do we have a narrow bandwidth of tolerable emotions and feel that heightened emotions interfere with productivity?

In chapter 3 we take a deeper look at depression. Chapters 7 through 11 provide several tools to help you overcome the defense mechanisms that you developed as a child and that now may hinder you from being as open and authentic as possible and attracting the type of love you crave.

Chapter 3

Your Mind:
A Resentment Factory

I believe that the root cause of most destructive and self-destructive behavior is resentment. When babies want to sleep and are forced to eat, that foments resentment. When children want to play and are told to do math, that foments resentment. When teenagers want to explore sexuality and are told that they cannot or should not, that foments resentment. When college students want to be artists and are told they must study to become doctors or lawyers or engineers, that foments resentment.

In addition, whenever we have expectations and "should have" or "should not have" statements floating around our minds, that foments resentment. For example: "I should not have been in that car accident," "My wife should not have cheated on me," "My dog should not have run away," "My parents should not have gotten divorced," "My mother should not have put me up for adoption," "I should not have been violated like that," "My ex-husband should not have taken so much money in the divorce," "I should have become a banker," "I should have bought that other house…" Any time we wish something were different about our pasts, that is a resentment.

If you look closely at all the behavior modification that goes on in America so that people can participate in society and not end up in prison or dispatched, you may agree that our society is an immense resentment factory. If you could measure the quantity of resentment and compare it to that of the gross domestic product, resentment would far surpass the GDP. I have met very few people who convincingly say, "My life has been perfect. I accept it 100 percent, including the things that were painful and that I didn't want or expect to occur." In fact, Herbert Spencer's notion (often incorrectly attributed to Darwin) of the "survival of the fittest," which fuels the "winner take all" hypercompetition of late capitalism, engenders resentment because the hedonic treadmill of the mind is insatiable. There is no end to consumer-based capitalism. There is no end to "conspicuous consumption," as Thorstein Veblen called it. One can never have too much. Keeping up with the Joneses is now a public sport like football or baseball. Have you ever heard the word *bling*?

One can never "do" enough either. One can never accomplish "too much," not even Bill Gates or Oprah Winfrey. People who are not constantly driven are thought of as slackers and deviants. Psychologically, the hypercompetitive nature of the American paradigm makes us feel as if *we are never good enough*, as if there is always more to accomplish, more to "do," more to watch, more to hear, more to taste, more to see, more to have, more places to visit...more more more more more.

Some people choose to rebel against the tacit edicts of our paradigm. Aside from the garden-variety malcontents, some people actually go out of their way to tell the world how upset they are with the way their lives have turned out. Some people drink too much, drive too fast, spend too much, eat too much, watch too much television, play too many video games, spend too much time on the internet (probably playing war games, gambling, checking their stock portfolios, and viewing pornography)... And these behaviors begin as compensations for our unmet primary needs. And when they fail to produce the desired results, people sometimes decide to turn up the volume. What is it that most of these people in our culture are trying to express? Is it something akin to the character Howard Beale's renowned statement in the 1976 movie *Network*: "I'm mad as hell and I'm not going to take it anymore!"? I believe that most rebels and nonconformists — some of whom have accomplished spectacular things before dying prematurely — are trying to say one thing: *I resent my childhood because I was not loved in the manner that I believe I should have been loved in.*

I noted in chapter 2 that, as sentient beings, what we want beyond survival and safety, more than anything else, is to be loved — and we wish to be loved *unconditionally*. Not admired. Not loved because we are rich or powerful or beautiful or sexy. Just loved. Just loved for being alive. But we are loved seemingly unconditionally for only an extremely brief period in our lives, when we are completely dependent on our caregivers and parents in order to survive. *And maybe not even then.*

As we grow up — or rather, as people in my generation grew up during the 1960s and 1970s — we received the positive reinforcement that we as children interpreted as love for doing things, acting in certain ways, performing certain tasks, accomplishing certain goals. This is why I consider America to be a resentment factory: even if you become the richest or most beautiful or most famous or most respected or most accomplished person and do everything right, when you finally gain the acceptance, positive reinforcement, love, and accolades that you have been yearning for, *you will either resent the people giving them because they made you jump through hoops like a dancing bear to get them, or you will not trust them, or you will think that you must now become even more rich or beautiful or accomplished in order to maintain that acceptance and love.* That is why people feel as if they are perpetually on hamster wheels and that nothing they do is ultimately good enough. This is why consumer-based capitalism is ground zero for resentment.

Did you ever notice that there are currently no courses in our public educational system on how to love and be loved? And yet intimacy correlates more strongly with happiness than earning or accumulating money does. But the goal of our educational system is not to produce happy adults; it is to produce diligent workers. Its main emphasis is how to teach children to successfully compete in the rat race, become productive members of society, climb to the top of the heap of busynesspeople, and be successful by society's definition — that is, earn inordinate amounts of money.

"He's very successful" was a euphemism for "He has a high net worth" even before *Pride and Prejudice.*

However, all of the behavior modification, negative feedback, and conditional positive reinforcement that goes into turning a child into a productive member of society creates resentment. Anyone who has worked a twelve-step program or attended a "transformational" or "personal-growth" seminar such as the Hoffman Process, Emotional Freedom Techniques, Kabbalah, and primal therapy, or those offered by Landmark, Avatar, Tony Robbins, and Lifespring, knows that one of the keys to happiness and success is to release our resentments. You may have heard the phrase "Resentment is like poking yourself in the eye and waiting for someone else to go blind." Or,

"Resentment is like drinking poison and waiting for someone else to get sick." I believe that that "someone else" is often a primary caregiver who withheld love from us, loved us conditionally, violated our innate sense of trust, and/or abandoned or betrayed us. But that person who existed when we were four days old or four weeks old or four years old or nine years old or fifteen years old is long gone. Maybe he or she is dead. And yet we are still poking ourselves in the eye and drinking poison. How much sense does that make? As I discuss in detail in chapter 9, there is only one way to walk through the fire of resentment and burn off the *woulda-shoulda-coulda-didn'ts* that the mind creates: forgiveness. As Lily Tomlin reportedly said, "Forgiveness means giving up all hope of having a better past."

We cannot go back and change our childhoods, so why do we waste time viewing them negatively or complaining about them? *Wishing something that we cannot change to be different is like trying to shove a square peg into a round hole. And our minds do this all day long.*

Releasing the resentments that our minds create entails forgiving people who disappointed or betrayed or even violated us. And ultimately we need to learn how to replace those resentments with gratitude. *Why not?* If we are walking, breathing, and thinking, if we got out of bed this morning, if we had food to eat today, if there is one person in our lives who listens to us, if we have roofs over our heads this evening, then there are things to be grateful for. One of the tools of cognitive behavioral therapy — writing gratitude lists — works because it subtly informs us that happiness is a choice, or that we can at least choose the lens through which we look or "change the station" playing on the radios in our heads. The cliché about the glass being half empty or half full is a cliché because it is true.

Every act of perception is subjective. For example, when asked who his greatest teacher is, His Holiness the Dalai Lama is expected to reply, "The Buddha." However, when I have seen him answer that question he replied, "The Chinese" — the people who ruthlessly slaughtered two million of his people. I was taught that when some Kabbalists in Auschwitz were led to be shot, they danced in order to thank God for giving them negative emotions to overcome. I myself, after twenty-five years, wrote a letter to the person who drove the car that almost killed me and caused me over forty hours of surgery, years of recovery, and a lifetime of scars, and forgave him. Most people hang on to their resentments as if they were life rafts in the middle of the ocean.

Unforgiveness — being unwilling to forgive — is our desire to share our suffering. If we are not willing to forgive someone, it simply means that we are not finished with suffering yet. Unacceptance of reality causes suffering. Pain does not cause suffering. Pain is immediate, and it usually diminishes with time. As the bumper sticker reads, "Pain is inevitable; suffering is optional." Since language creates our reality, please try on a semantic distinction between pain and suffering: pain is immediate and informs our body that something needs to be addressed imminently. If we have a broken arm, the pain informs us to stop thinking about what we might eat for dinner or how fantastic our last vacation in Hawaii was. Pain is information. It directs all of our attention to a problem that must be remedied. If we have a toothache, that means there is a situation, probably a cavity or an inflamed nerve, that must be addressed. The pain will grow until it becomes insufferable (pun intended) and we have no choice but to fix the problem. Pain does not cause suffering; what causes suffering is an intolerance of pain. In our culture we do not have a great relationship with pain. For the purposes of this book, we need to distinguish between pain and suffering. If we wish to change our glasses from half empty to half full, then we have to give up our resentments, embrace our entire lives, be grateful for all of the gifts we receive and freedoms we enjoy, and not allow our minds to create suffering by nonacceptance, by making us think we are "not good enough" or that we will "be happy when we accomplish X in the future."

If this sounds easy, it is not. It is the most difficult thing we will ever attempt, because it means a change in personal identity. And then it requires enrolling everyone in our lives in our new identities. And we fear change. We have gotten used to our narratives, are familiar with the pros and cons, and may even subconsciously enjoy the benefits of playing the role of victim or hero, of sucking other people into our dramas, exacting empathy, and so on. Change means uncertainty and we live in a culture that prefers the devil we know.

A larger problem is that *many of us would not know who we were if we gave up our resentments.* That is why the process is arduous, why there is no quick fix, no hack for it. Well, yes, there is a hack: the hack is authenticity, but it takes time for authenticity to bear fruit. Authenticity requires daily practice — deciding who we are and what tools we will employ to be that person. And that is what this book is devoted to: to providing tools to change our perspectives. The past is dead and gone; the future does not yet exist. We cannot change either of them. But we can change the story about the past that our mind created, or at least the judgments that our mind added to that story; and we can mitigate our expectations about the future. For every time our mind tells us: "I will be happy when...," what we are really saying is: "I do not accept my life today and who I am. I want things to be different from the way they are."

I believe that what we call a midlife crisis is really a questioning of personal identity that occurs when someone accomplishes many of the things he or she set out to accomplish but fails to attain the happiness he or she expected to accompany having 2.3 children, a home/mortgage, two automobile leases, luxurious vacations, and so on. Popular culture — films, songs, television, books, magazines, and countless websites, apps, and social media — teaches us that if we attract a spouse, earn excessive amounts of money, buy a home or homes, and raise children, we will be happy. But after accomplishing these things, many people are not happy. They are simply unhappy parents and homeowners with countless stresses, financial obligations, and perennial pressures weighing on them such as leases, mortgages, credit card bills, and student loans. Then they feel betrayed. The voice in their heads asks, "Wasn't accomplishing all these things supposed to make me happy?" But there is no end to the hedonic treadmill, since children, houses, cars, boats, and wardrobes appear to be in constant need of expensive upkeep.

It is possible, though, to shift our paradigms and perceptions. If we would like to alter our perceptions, the first thing to do is to analyze our frame — the way we were taught to view reality and accept what society (law, ethics, religion) tells us is good and bad, good and evil, right and wrong, correct and incorrect, order and disorder, ease and disease, and so on. As Jiddu Krishnamurti famously said, "It is no measure of health to be well adjusted to a profoundly sick society." Western culture can be viewed as a matrix of beliefs buttressed by capitalism, science, and religion.

America was founded on the inalienable right to pursue happiness, which meant having the freedom to believe what we want to believe religiously. But we have learned so much in the past 250 years. Consciousness has evolved in so many interesting ways — we have new understandings of reality thanks to quantum physics, philosophy, psychology, medicine, technology, and so on. And Americans today enjoy more freedoms and privileges than most human beings who ever walked on planet Earth. So why is it so difficult to attain and maintain happiness? I believe it is due to the fact that in our culture *we are taught to desire the wrong things.* So even if we attain them, any happiness they bring is relatively brief. We are consciously and subconsciously taught that if we behave in a certain manner, do certain things, and accomplish certain goals, we will be loved. Yet anyone who believes that he would like to have "Accomplished Much," "Worked Really Hard," or "Richest Guy in This Cemetery" on his tombstone, rather than "Beloved," is insane. Why do so many people brag or complain about how hard they work?

Maybe it is time to reframe the way we see afflictions and the poor or impulsive or misguided choices people make. Maybe when people become catatonic, it is really a signpost that reads, "I do not feel loved unconditionally." Maybe when someone drinks a bottle of tequila and drives fast around a crowded city, it is a signpost that reads, "I don't want to act like a dancing bear anymore in an effort to be loved."? Maybe when someone goes $4,078 in credit card debt (the average for American individuals), it is a signpost that reads, "I feel I have to buy more more more in order to be accepted and loved by others"? *Is it possible that many of the things we consider to be afflictions are actually signposts, or cries for help, from people who want to feel they are loved and lovable, who have negative or critical voices in their heads telling them they are not good enough, that their lives should be other than the way they are?*

The ultimate manifestation of resentment — usually after the self-destructive and destructive signposts go unread by others — is suicide. Only a small percentage of people who attempt suicide suffer from so much physical pain that self-euthanasia is a logical choice. For the vast majority of people who try to kill themselves, I believe that their ultimate subconscious goal is to be heard. Unfortunately, they have tried for so long to get people to hear them — usually by drinking, causing car accidents, egregious spending, and eating and fornicating beyond their means — that they feel they have only one resort left: emotional terrorism.

However, the messages of emotional terrorists get quickly lost in the medium. As a psychotherapist, I have observed that, like terrorists, most people who suffer from suicidal ideation are yearning to be heard. If you listen carefully, you will find that most are saying something similar: "I do not feel loved in the manner I believe I should be loved — namely, *unconditionally*." Unfortunately, the message gets lost, because suicidal ideation is a supposed symptom of clinical depression, which is a mental disorder. But I do not see it that way. I believe that we want to be loved; our minds create resentments about not being loved unconditionally; we get tired of jumping through hoops in order to gain what we mistake to be love (see "midlife crisis"), so we self-soothe, self-medicate, act out, lead double lives, have afflictions, drive too fast, spend too much, drink too much, eat too much, or check out with a debilitating form of "depression." Sometimes it gets so bad that suicide seems like the only way out. But nobody was born with negative thoughts in his or her head. And negative thoughts do not appear ex nihilo. So how did negative, hypercritical self-talk infiltrate our culture? And how did it become pathologized into a mental disorder? What is it about highly competitive capitalism that causes us to feel good enough and worthy only in snatches?

Have you ever heard of someone going into a psychologist's office and saying, "I truly feel loved, appreciated, and respected by my friends, family members, and coworkers, and I am depressed"? *Depression is an understandable default reaction for anyone who does not want to deal with the stresses and pressures of modern life, who feels alienated, unconnected, disconnected, poorly connected, unloved, and possibly unlovable.* This is why transformational seminars, self-help books, and twelve-step meetings work: they teach people how to love or at least accept themselves and their lives, how to release their resentment at not being loved unconditionally, and how to feel heard without resorting to erecting egregious signposts such as alcoholism, debt, putative mental illness, physical illness, or other signals that people use when acting out in an effort to be heard by others.

What I have learned from being a psychotherapist is that we all need to feel as if our emotions are valid, that we are not crazy for feeling and thinking certain things. And this interaction does not transpire via text messaging. We need to be face-to-face with people, we need to share communal experiences with others, we need to break bread and connect with other people who can reflect back to us acceptance and love and make us feel heard. This is why talk therapy is a respite from the highly judgmental rat race. I recall a psychology professor describing his understanding of clinical psychotherapy as follows: "My job is to lease my emotions in fifty-minute intervals." That connection with another human being, someone who is not judging us, can be essential to overcoming the negative voices in our heads.

I believe that much of what we consider to be mental illness is really just thoughts, feelings, and actions that do not promote *productivity* or participation as workers in our society; that resentment is caused by wanting to be loved unconditionally but possessing only tools to gain love conditionally; that acting out or becoming mentally "disordered" is really a message in a bottle, placed there by a person who hopes someone will see it and save/love him or her; that psychiatry and psychology are fantastic for diagnosing and treating the myriad symptoms/manifestations (messages in bottles) of resentment — mostly by covering them with Band-Aids (pharmaceuticals that mask the negative emotions). But the root problems often remain untreated, and ultimately the Band-Aids fall off. Again, the subconscious root problem for many people is: "I was not loved in the manner I believe I should have been loved in — *namely, unconditionally.*"

Depression and many of the diseases and afflictions listed in the current edition of the *Diagnostic and Statistical Manual of Mental Disorders* — which is what the insurance companies consult when determining whether to pay for doctors' visits and medicines — should be considered undesirable only within the frame of our highly competitive capitalistic society that stresses us out because we continually think that we must accomplish and buy things in order to gain love. As a society we are addicted to busyness and the feeling that enough is never enough. The light at the end of the tunnel keeps moving further and further away. Desire, as we will see in chapter 8, is insatiable. Personally, I believe that it is more precise to discuss the symptoms of depression as un-ease or uneasiness than dis-ease or disease. Depression and many other disorders named by our culture are our bodies' default modalities that allow us to escape from the productivity paradigm and cease being judged by people living within that frame. People exhibit symptoms of depression because they are tired of not feeling connected, not feeling loved, not feeling lovable, and because they are tired of failing at their attempts to gain acceptance, approval, and love.

To release our resentment about not being loved unconditionally, the greatest tool we can use is to forgive everyone unequivocally. Our parents and teachers and siblings and relatives and friends did the best they could with the tools they had at the time, so we must forgive them. Period. Unforgiveness manifests as resentment or absurdly wanting things we cannot change to change. We only cause our own suffering when we do not embrace every moment of childhood and who we are today. Leonard Cohen so aptly wrote, "We are not mad, we are human, we want to love, and someone must forgive us for the paths we take to love, for the paths are many and dark, and we are ardent and cruel in our journey." The goal of this book is to help us become conscious of each of our individual paths and provide new tools for procuring the unconditional love we crave, so that we can avoid being ardent and cruel — to ourselves and others — on our journeys.

Chapter 4

The Myth of Romance

The narratives that we consider to be "normal," if not inspiring, about romantic love greatly affect our consciousness and how we relate to others. We need to examine how romance has evolved over the past millennium to see how it affects our mental lives. It is possible that all great narratives in literature, music, film, theater, and television revolve around conflict, challenges, and overcoming internal and external obstacles. The myth of romantic love is a good example. In *Love in the Western World*, first published in French in 1939, Denis de Rougemont proposes that romantic love as we know it today is particular to Western civilization, a relatively recent development (thirteenth century), and that it usually entails something illicit or forbidden. Robert A. Johnson, in *We: Understanding the Psychology of Romantic Love*, extrapolated from de Rougemont's theories to state that romantic love is not conducive to long-lasting, psychologically healthy relationships. Although passionate love affairs make us feel vibrant and "alive," de Rougemont and Johnson viewed passion negatively. De Rougemont believed that in passion we subconsciously seek suffering; contrary to what many of us believe, passion is not conducive to healthy, harmonious, functional marriages.

How do most romantic couples find and show love and affection, as portrayed in film, television programs, literature (romance novels in particular), and music? Most find love by overcoming what seem to be insurmountable obstacles — he is rich and she is poor, or the reverse; or he is black and she is white, or the reverse; one of them is already married to someone else; one of them is deeply wounded by a previous relationship (abandonment or betrayal) and unable or unwilling to engage again; and so on. Romantic films, television programs, and literature generally end in one of three ways: tragic, comic, or bittersweet. In tragedies, one or both of the lovers die; in comedies the lovers ride or drive into the sunset together; bittersweet narratives are mélanges of tragedy and comedy — more subtly nuanced — and usually leave audiences with more questions than answers. Think European art-house films. Traditional tragedies and comedies imply that the passion is eternal, that the couples, or at least their ideal, will last forever. In comedies (happy endings) the credits roll before the romance can grow stale; in tragedies the relationship is decimated by a death or two so that the ideal of eternal passion can endure. Romantic American films usually subtly censor the mundane parts of lovers' lives, such as taking out the trash (except to sneak a cigarette or donut), washing dishes, putting on their socks, or conducting most quotidian activities. When we see lovers together, they are usually overcoming internal and external obstacles to their being together, and then rejoicing with seemingly unbounded passion. Is it possible that as a culture we conflate sex and love? We subconsciously assume when we watch a couple make love at the end of a comedy or the beginning of a tragedy that they will be together forever. However, there is no *Pretty Woman II*. Nor is there *Titanic: The Sequel* or *Thelma and Louise Ride Again*.

The brave knights of feudal lore engendered an ideal of courtly love for the wives of the lords they protected. This courtly love was never consummated; it remained an ideal, and never became sexual, because of the knightly code of honor. The knights worshipped the fair ladies as symbols of beauty, a type of courtly love that actually condemned passion. But as we already know, rules were made to be broken. Take the Garden of Eden as a parallel: the one thing that God specifically tells Adam and Eve not to do, they are tricked into doing. *Could it be that taboos and prohibitions actually cause objects to be desired?* De Rougemont notes that we can clearly trace the theme of adultery as passion in popular literature. If you think about all the films and television programs you have ever seen, can you name five passionate love affairs between carefree happily married couples? (I mean happily married to *each other*.) How about two? We desire whatever is illicit. If someone says, "Don't do X," it may immediately make X titillating, enticing.

Is it possible that when given the opportunity to have a peaceful, calm, and harmonious relationship, some people subconsciously create obstructions that prohibit or hinder themselves from being united with their beloved? Have you ever had a friend who yearned to get married and, soon after doing so, immersed himself or herself so deeply in work that the marriage became dysfunctional? Are there links between passion, suffering, and drama? If Capulet had condoned or actually desired Juliet's marriage to Romeo, what would the young lovers' story have been? Would they have lived happily ever after?

Interestingly, de Rougemont claims that "what they [lovers] need is not one another's presence, but one another's absence."

Why does absence make the heart grow fonder?

Why do long-distance relationships seem more passionate than conventional marriages?

Is it possible that our culture mistakes lust for love? (It would help explain why 40 percent of marriages end in divorce.)

Is it possible that we lust after things only because religion has made sex dirty, evil, shameful, illegal, and even sometimes punishable by death?

Johnson writes, "Romantic love is the single greatest energy system in the Western psyche. In our culture, it has supplanted religion as the arena in which men and women seek meaning, transcendence, wholeness, and ecstasy." Both marriage and divorce are billion-dollar industries. So is the film industry. So is the music industry. So is the romance novel industry. All of them rely on the myth of romantic love, the archetypal Western romance, to earn countless dollars. Modern lovers often delude themselves into believing that the ultimate meaning of life can be found in another human being, the "missing part" of themselves. Try this narrative on for size: many people in Western civilization think that they are inherently unwhole; through popular culture we come to believe that the missing part of us is "out there" somewhere in the form of a soul mate; once we locate our soul mate, we will be whole. Any obstacle such as physical distance or the threat of discovery by a jealous husband, wife, or fiancé — or asteroids or ships going down or World War III or bank robberies or car chases or terrible diseases or fires or floods — only redoubles our impassioned quest and makes us feel truly alive! "You complete me," says Tom Cruise to Renée Zellweger in the 1996 film *Jerry Maguire*

as he struggles to start his new career and she helps him overcome obstacle after obstacle.

Are we so enveloped by the myth of romantic love that we
cannot understand there are other types of love that may be
more conducive to marriage than the love we assume correlates
with sexual passion?

Do we mistake passion or intense recreational sex for love
when the relationship between passion and love could be more
complex or even nonexistent?

When we watch pornography do we think, "Oh, that is so
sweet! They really love each other!"?

Despite the fleeting ecstasy that we feel when we are supposedly in the throes of passion, we spend much time feeling
a deep sense of loneliness, alienation, and frustration over our
inability to make genuinely loving and committed attachments.
Usually we blame other people for failing or being incompetent
in some way. But maybe we subconsciously create problems in
or sabotage or implode our relationships. It rarely occurs to
us that we need to change our own unconscious attitudes —
the expectations and demands we impose on relationships and
other people. Maybe 40 percent of marriages in America end
in divorce because we conflate lust and love, and when the lust
wanes people assume that the love must be gone too?

Very few long-lasting, committed, functional, relatively
peaceful monogamous relationships are perpetually passionate
— yet what we learned about relationships from the stories we
read as adolescents and young adults would lead us to believe
that without passion there is no intimacy. The reason passion
does not last is because, when we subconsciously objectify our
lovers as the missing parts of us, and they eventually sneeze or
burp, we subconsciously realize that they are their own entities

and, hence, cannot be the missing parts of us. "When a man's projections on a woman unexpectedly evaporate, he will announce that he is 'disenchanted' with her; he is disappointed that she is a human being rather than the embodiment of his fantasy," writes Robert Johnson.

Look at the most popular romantic films, books, and songs of the last hundred years, and you will find that most are about lovers overcoming obstacles to being in a passionate relationship. But could the polar opposite actually be more accurate — that overcoming obstacles foments that desire and appreciation? If two people were absolutely ideal as partners but had no worries, would they find the other person less attractive? "There is just no chemistry" or "I am just not attracted to her" is what we hear after a friend describes someone as the perfect partner but then discovers there are no obstacles. So what are people really trying to express through all this sexuality? Is it love? A desire to be loved? Is it power? Lust? Possession? Frustration? Hate? Revenge? Or is it mere distraction? Or all of the above? *Obviously it is not possible for an entire civilization to be so misguided as to be driven by lust, power, money, possession, and war, but how is what we consider to be "normal" working out for us?* What is "healthy" sexuality when people are consciously trying to avoid producing a child? What are people trying to express when they want to have recreational sex with someone else?

Consider this anonymous quote: "If sex were so satisfying...you would only have to do it once."

In his book *Constructing the Sexual Crucible: An Integration of Sexual and Marital Therapy*, David Schnarch posits that sexual intercourse in America has become akin to mutual masturbation, that the way we approach recreational sex is too goal oriented, too focused on orgasm; for some couples, then, intercourse has become more like a business transaction than a mindful, loving, connective, passionate, intimate experience. In a lecture I attended, Esther Perel opined that passionate, intimate sex and marriage may unwittingly be mutually exclusive, because "how can you desire what you already have?"

I categorize sex as either procreational, in which the goal is to produce a baby, or nonprocreational or recreational, in which producing a baby is intentionally avoided (controlled). What, then, is the purpose of sex and the infinite space it occupies in our collective unconscious and individual consciousnesses when people are not making babies? And what is this elusive thing called "passion" that we yearn for?

If aliens traveled here from another galaxy to observe us and wanted to know how human beings procreate, they would have no problem finding out. There is nothing more natural than making a baby. However, if aliens typed "sex" into Google, I think they would be bemused by the sexual activities our species engages in when we are not procreating. The first question they might pose is: "Recreational sex seems to have become very athletic. Do some people consider it a form of calisthenics, a.k.a. sexercise?" Then, I believe, they would find the employment of masturbation as a sleep aid, a meditation, a warm-up act, or a "release" from the daily stresses, disappointments, and traumas of highly competitive capitalism to be somewhat bizarre, imprudent, and alarming. Lastly, I believe they would ask, "Is there a concrete relationship between sex, intimacy, and love? And what are the ideal circumstances and conditions that create lasting passionate love or loving compassionate passion?"

As I noted in chapter 1, in the story about what the

professor's wife feels when she has an orgasm, our minds project our own bodily pleasures onto our partners' bodies. This is completely misguided. Just because you or I enjoy having our necks kissed in a certain way or our arms stroked in a certain manner does not mean that anyone else does. Any assumptions regarding what pleases or displeases the bodies of other human beings are fallacious. The only way to bridge this chasm is through authentic communications and loving, compassionate explorations. Also, we must recognize that our bodies and what pleases them will change over time, and that the same will happen to our partner's bodies and what pleases them. This could be called personal "sexual evolution," and it is a good thing since we preternaturally crave novelty. As a species we get bored rather easily — usually after eight years, the average lifespan of marriages that end in divorce. The activities we once considered illicit will become more and more titillating over time (mostly owing to the fact that we considered them verboten), and we may eventually become drawn to them like a moth to a flame. Please forgive the mixed metaphor, but once we partake of the forbidden fruit, we will most likely become addicted or repulsed or both (more about that in chapter 6). This is how the mind functions.

What can we do to avoid the traps and clichés of the Western paradigm and explore radically mindful, loving, connective, passionate, intimate experiences that may or may not include nonprocreative sex? Here is what I recommend trying:

- Acknowledge that there is no inherent relationship between sex, intimacy, and love, and that any assumptions you make will probably end up ruining whatever connection you are trying to create.

- Have open conversations about what your partner considers to be loving and pleasurable signs of affection.
- Forget everything you have ever learned about sex from other people and anything about sex you have ever seen in the media and on the internet.
- Be committed to being vulnerable — risky is risqué.
- Create a physical environment in which you can feel free to be physically naked without distractions (such as nosy neighbors or police officers).
- Create the mental space you need so that you can be mentally naked and present (and release the fears you learned in the past and expectations about the imminent future).
- Create the emotional space you need to be emotionally naked and open.
- For theists, create the spiritual space you need to be spiritually open to connecting with and being intimate with a fellow human being (and open to letting whatever is divine in you touch whatever is divine in your partner).
- Disregard any techniques or anything previously learned from human bodies, including your own.
- Have a sense of wonder and explore with unbiased curiosity. Or more precisely, be as present as humanly possible and do your utmost to attune yourself to how your partner is breathing and moving and feeling at that very moment. If you catch your mind wandering forward or backward or sideways, gently guide it back to focusing on sensations in your hands, lips, and other sensitive body parts.

I hope that some of your assumptions regarding romance, sex, love, and relationships have been challenged by this chapter. There are many ways of organizing societies, and although the married-for-life, male-female model has been in place for thousands of years, I am unpersuaded that the Judeo-Christian notion of a nuclear family will last much longer.

A large portion of our mental lives is devoted to relationships — *and rightly so*. But if we already have concrete models in mind regarding what we believe these relationships should resemble, then how authentic can we be? Spend a few minutes reflecting on how your assumptions about relationships have actually ended up causing the destruction of relationships. If we are not aware of our expectations regarding relationships and cannot communicate them, then we are inviting dysfunctionality and drama.

I realize that propriety dictates that I put business before pleasure, but for the purposes of this book I thought it best to invert them. Let's now move on from discussing romantic love to the other insatiable consumer of much of our mental lives: business.

Chapter 5

Taking Care of Busyness

America's not a country. It's just a business.
— JACKIE IN *Killing Them Softly*

Spending the majority of our waking hours naked in a jungle searching for food and trying not to be eaten by lions and tigers would make us extremely authentic. Our minds would be laser-focused, and we would have no time to be depressed. But humans have evolved and created relatively safe, secure societies where we no longer have to search for food or worry about being eaten. We have governments that protect us and enable us to spend our days conducting business and earning money. It appears, however, that some people get their sense of self, their personal identity, from a perverse game of consumerism and conspicuous consumption that relates to their occupation. Let's take a brief look at how capitalism has evolved over the past few hundred years and how it affects the ways we think.

The Pilgrims came to America to pursue their religious beliefs unencumbered, or at least less encumbered, by government. In terms of mapping out land, establishing colonies, finding and growing food as well as tobacco and other crops to trade, and having ample natural supplies for building shelters, the Pilgrims were probably lucky to have landed on such fertile soil and vast resources. How many of us would spend sixty-six days crossing the Atlantic on the Mayflower in order to practice another variation of a religion? Many of us would not defer gratification for fifteen minutes just to get a second marshmallow, so I am fairly certain that risking death on a wooden sailing ship on a treacherous sea for two months would be anathema to the majority. Look how much people's conviction waned between 1620 and almost 2020. What are most Americans — not including those in the armed forces — willing to die for today? What do you think of the adage "If there is nothing worth dying for, then there is nothing worth living for"? What would any of us risk our lives for today? After we have reached a certain level of creature comfort, what would make us sufficiently uncomfortable that we would be willing to die today? Would we risk our lives...

- so that our children would receive an education?
- so that our family would have land to farm?
- so that people in our community could build a church?
- so that our sons could work in a factory for minimum wage?
- so that our daughters could fight in the army?
- so that other people could express their political views, even if those views are abhorrent to us?
- to build roads and bridges for other people?
- to establish military outposts in the Philippines or replace governments in Iraq or Afghanistan?

How many of us would endure what our parents, grand-parents, or great-grandparents endured to come to America and become Americans? Much of the time, fathers or sons came to America first, earned money, and sent it back so that the rest of the family could immigrate. Have you ever chat-ted with a foreign taxi driver in Manhattan or a foreign laborer picking vegetables in Ventura County? During the exactly one hundred years since my grandparents immigrated to America, things have not changed much. America remains one of the most desirable places in the world to live — *and rightly so*. It definitely embodies the finest ideals for freedom and opportu-nity on our planet.

In 1791 the First Amendment to the United States Constitu-tion was ratified. It concerned the freedom of speech, press, re-ligion, and petition and reads as follows: "Congress shall make no law respecting an establishment of religion, or prohibiting the free exercise thereof; or abridging the freedom of speech, or of the press; or the right of the people peaceably to assemble, and to petition the Government for a redress of grievances." The Constitution and its amendments are some of the princi-ples that make America one of the greatest places on earth to live. But what is it really like in America? Is it a true meritoc-racy? Is there equality of opportunity? How do we measure things such as opportunity, freedom of speech, merit, success, happiness? How do individuals get their sense of self and per-sonal identity in our culture? Is there an active countercultural movement today tantamount to, say, the one that rallied against the Vietnam War in the early 1970s? How have social media influenced our lives and how we present ourselves? How have social media like Facebook and Twitter influenced politics and business? Is living in America different for men and women?

What about for black people and white people? Asians? Mexicans? Pakistanis? How have our attitudes toward authority evolved, changed, or shifted over the past 250 years? These are some of the questions I address in this chapter.

Shortly after America was attacked on 9/11, President George W. Bush told Americans to "go shopping." I study consciousness and so I have looked at the way capitalism and money/banking affect how we think and what we think about. In *Money Changes Everything: How Finance Made Civilization Possible*, William N. Goetzmann writes, "Finance has increasingly made us creatures of time." The past no longer exists and the future does not yet exist, so how is it that our attention is so frequently directed at potential future scenarios that may or may not arise into existence? What does it say about our beliefs about the future when the average individual credit card debt is $4,078 according to www.TheBalance.com? What does it say about us that the national average for a mortgage is $222,261, according to www.LendingTree.com? Are there many other societies where people can walk into a bank and walk out a few hours later owing $222,261 to be paid over the next thirty years? In a lecture I attended, Ken Dychtwald stated that the vast majority of human beings who existed on planet Earth never lived to be forty years old; so what is in the minds of the 11–26 million Americans who apply for thirty-year mortgages every year?

Currently, our government has borrowed $19.8 trillion, and we are the beneficiaries of this debt as distributed to us via banks in the form of mortgages, credit cards, and student loans. What if, 250 years ago, someone knocked on our doors and said, "We think it would be good for our community to build schools, hospitals, roads, libraries, a police force, a fire brigade, and an army...and the total bill comes to $10,000. Your share will be $333 a year in taxes. How does that sound?" Most of us would be in favor of what we consider to be indicators of civilization — schools, hospitals, libraries, roads, police, and so on. So why has our government had to borrow $19.8 trillion to pay for our basic amenities?

Most Americans agree that assuming some debt to buy a home or car or pay for college is not terrible. *Debt — or betting that the future will be more abundant than the present — has been as profitable to our country as slavery and war have been.* Banking as a métier has been ridiculously prosperous for so many of my University of Pennsylvania classmates. In terms of consciousness, we think in terms of "investments," and investments are like trees that take time to bloom and bear fruit. If Americans thought only about the present, and were able to pay attention to the present moment, then there would be no need for what *Time* magazine called the "Mindful Revolution." Alas, we apparently spend such a great portion of our mental lives cogitating over and rehearsing imagined future situations that we actually need a billion-dollar mindfulness industry to teach us how to be present, to help us relearn how to be here now.

Americans also would agree that capitalism — originally based on the notion of "survival of the fittest" — is the most efficient system for weeding out inferior products and getting the best products to market at the fairest prices. The forces of supply and demand in a free market ensure that consumers get the best products at the best prices as corporations vie for our business. These were obviously revolutionary concepts after feudalism, as our society discovered steel, learned how to make guns, and became industrialized, as we shifted from concentrating on agriculture to manufacturing, to mass production, to modern urban life.

What exactly is a free market? A truly "free market" with absolutely no regulations is when I offer to sell you a carrot, you fatally stab me in the neck, take the carrot, boil it along with my pets, and enslave my family. That would be a free market without rules or regulations. In Western civilization, however, we have regulations — also known as laws — prohibiting murder, thievery, and slavery. However, *once human beings taste power, they tend to support rules and regulations that benefit themselves rather than protect the rights, freedoms, and opportunities of everyone else.* E.g., the history of white males. In terms of studying consciousness, it appears historically that consciousness adjusts to new "normals" more rapidly than we think — or, more precisely, in the words of Lord Acton: "Power corrupts. Absolute power corrupts absolutely." As noted previously, if in 1770 someone knocked on our door to collect taxes for protection, our children's education, the safety and health of our families, and so on, we would have happily handed it over. In just 250 years taxes have become a *burden*.

Although as a collective we may agree that taxes must be paid and that a $19.8 trillion government spending deficit is unsustainable, I believe that individually we dislike paying taxes and have come to believe that a mythical "someone else" will cover our individual shares. Specifically, almost every American I have ever met expects someone else to pay for the privileges and freedoms that we enjoy. I have never heard anyone, not even Warren Buffett, say, "Hey, I enjoy safety from bombings, fires, pillaging, and robbers 365 days a year; my family uses public schools, hospitals, roads, safe water, libraries, and national parks...so I've decided to pay a little extra on my tax return this year!" The federal and state governments hand us bills every April for the money they spend on us, and without fail we tell them that they spent too much, spent it inefficiently, and we are going to deduct whatever we can from the full bill, pay less, do whatever is legally possible to lessen this burden. Hence our government's $19.8 trillion operating deficit. I argue that the psychological reason for this is that most of our interactions with authority come in the form of traffic tickets, parking tickets, and city, state, and federal taxes. That's why we take schools, roads, libraries, and hospitals for granted. In just 250 years Americans have grown to subconsciously mistrust government and hate authority. We have adjusted to not experiencing war on our soil, to not having mass riots and murders, to sending our children to relatively safe public schools, and to a "normal" personal safety that is probably the highest in the world.

Primacy has always been given to property owners in our country — originally they were the only people who had the right to vote. But what does it mean to "own" property? When you die, do you still own the property? If an earthquake, tsunami, or hurricane destroys that swath of planet Earth, then what do you own? Humans were nomadic for most of our time on earth; staying stationary entered our consciousness only during the agricultural revolution. For most of history we lived in tribes consisting of extended family members. Only since the Industrial Revolution have people left their families and congregated in urban areas to find work. "Owning" a portion of the planet seems to mean that the local government issues you a piece of paper stating that a particular patch is temporarily yours to do a limited number of things on. If you think about it, does it seem like human beings can "own" land? And yet homeownership on a stationary piece of earth as deeded by the local government (and borrowing an average of $222,261 to purchase that deed) remains an integral part of our economy and the American dream.

More recently, how have computers, smartphones, the internet, and social media affected our attention and our consciousness? Does having infinite information at our fingertips twenty-four hours a day help us sleep soundly, or does it overwhelm us and stress us out? Could there be a correlation between the rise in depression and anxiety and the amount of time that the average person spends in front of an electronic device each day? Is there not something perversely Pavlovian about receiving vibrations and/or other stimuli intermittently throughout the day? And yet it is almost impossible to be a "productive" member of society without a smartphone, which in fact is just a small computer, camera, phone, calculator, GPS, calendar, messenger, music player, and so on, on your person or in your bag at all times. Is it possible not to be in fight-or-flight mode when urgent pings, pops, rings, and dings are intermittently shocking us throughout the day in the same way that, as scientists have demonstrated, such alarms drive laboratory rats insane?

Before we blindly accept diagnoses regarding our psychological and emotional well-being, it behooves us to question the frame in which diagnoses such as depression and anxiety were created. Our notions of success — such as owning property, having a 401K plan, and retiring at sixty-five years of age — are culturally contingent. Moreover, exponential advances in technology are obviously affecting both the way we think and the way we interact with each other. And borrowing vast sums of money for school, home, and maintaining a particular lifestyle is a type of commitment that could also be extremely stressful. Some might even see it as a self-imposed prison

— especially if our job is not our true calling, does not feed our heart and soul, and we are trapped in golden handcuffs. Such a situation might provoke both depression and anxiety. When treating people who take antidepressants in order to show up for jobs that do not nourish their hearts and souls, I often ask them who they are trying to please by being on the hamster wheel or hedonic treadmill known as the American dream. Usually it is their parents, who may even be long gone.

Similarly, when we can choose between having an experience, learning something new, expanding our horizons, or buying a material possession (especially one that takes ten to thirty years to pay off), we must realize that experiences, learning, and growing always trump material possessions. Studies show that on our deathbeds we will remember strolling the streets of Paris, but we will not remember baubles or anything else we ever bought or anyone bought for us. Nobody wants "Owned Several Properties," "Vacationed at Elite Resorts," or "Used to Wear Designer Clothing" on his or her tombstone.

Is consumerism addictive, like video games are? Do brands take advantage of, or create, our seemingly insatiable desires for more, better, different? Is it possible that once our necessities are taken care of, shopping is a sport? And do Instagram and other social media, which allow people to parade their victories for all the world to see, simply induce more consumerism? As I mentioned earlier, we should entertain the possibility that we are taught (mostly subconsciously) to want the wrong things. Here is how it happens: we see other people in the media (films, television, internet, social media) who appear to be happy or at least happier than we are, and we assume that those other people are happier because of the material possessions on or around them. Why are there so many television programs about celebrities' "cribs" and the lifestyles of the rich and famous? Why do characters in movies always live in luxurious homes beyond their means filled with highly visible brand-name products and drink particular beverages and drive particular cars?

It appears that humans naturally group themselves into more and more elite circles and define themselves by who they associate with and who they exclude from their inner circles. Our minds are insatiable: they constantly seek more, better, different. Thus, we have the choice either to constantly buy more stuff to feed the hungry ghost, or to retrain our minds.

Finally, is America really a meritocracy where everyone has the same freedoms and opportunities as everyone else? Do we have a free press? Is our government a true representative democracy with one vote per person, or do political action committees, wealthy campaign donors, and corporations have undue influence on our government? I believe that although our country was founded on the highest of ideals, after only 250 years we may have run amok, run aground, gone awry. Again, e.g., white males. *It seems as if the concept or myth of meritocracy has become a way of controlling people, of making them work harder and harder for less and less, making them feel that it is their own fault when they do not "succeed" (i.e., get rich).* And this myth of meritocracy is so powerful that it even makes people vote against their own interests.

Previous cultures "worked to live," and people in other places in the world still "work to live"; in America people "live to work," with those who are employed full-time reportedly working an average of forty-seven hours, or six days, a week, according to Gallup. And according to Robert Reich, in his book *Supercapitalism*, Americans have the least amount of vacation time of any civilized nation, and most Americans do not even take their allotted one or two weeks a year — mainly for fear that their jobs will not be there for them upon their return. "Working to live" means that people work thirty-five hours a week and earn enough money to disconnect themselves from their jobs, take three to six weeks of paid vacation, go to museums, go to plays and symphonies, take an occasional course to learn something they always dreamed of learning, play with their children, enjoy the national parks, see friends and relatives, read the newspaper, go for a jog, make love to their partners, and so on. According to Ruth Whippman in *America the Anxious: How Our Pursuit of Happiness Is Creating a Nation of Nervous Wrecks*, the average American spends four minutes a day socializing. Is it any wonder that Americans are more anxious and stressed out than ever before? If we enjoy more privileges and freedoms and protections than most other countries, then why aren't we the happiest? Maybe it is because the measures of success in our culture end up making us feel alienated and alone, as Robert Putnam proposes in *Bowling Alone*. I like what Bob Dylan said about success: "A man is a success if he gets up in the morning and gets to bed at night, and in between he does what he wants to do."

We need to question what we were taught would make us happy: did we learn from the narratives of films, songs, television, and literature that having passionate love affairs would make us happy? Were we taught that having one partner for life would make us happy? Did we learn that having millions of dollars in our bank accounts would make us happy? Did we learn that driving sports cars or boats or having expensive accoutrements would bring happiness? Because it turns out the one thing that correlates with happiness is the quality of our intimate relationships, how much we can depend on other people, and how securely we are able to connect with other people. Isn't it ironic that the supposed prizes of our brand of capitalism pull us apart and push us into big houses with fences, exclusive first-class lounges, country clubs, private boxes at sporting events and concerts, and so on? And maybe once people taste exclusivity they become unwilling to share it, they want to keep it exclusive so that they can believe they worked hard to earn it, or that God loves them, or some other myth or fictional subconscious narrative? No sane person wants "Worked Really Hard" on his or her tombstone, yet every day I hear people respond to the question "How are you?" with: "Crazybusy!" which obviously makes no sense since *crazybusy* describes *what* one is doing, not *how* one is doing.

I am not advocating slackerism; I am advocating balance. And being truthful about our life situations. I am advocating that each of us derives our personal identity from who we are, not what we own, where we vacation, or what we do to earn money. If we believe Malcolm Gladwell, then we agree that Steve Jobs and Bill Gates would not have become Steve Jobs or Bill Gates had either of them not been born in 1955, hit high school the same year that mainframe computers entered high schools, and had ten thousand leisure hours to obsessively tinker with hardware systems and design software for those devices.

Maybe it is time to unlearn "living to work" and relearn "working to live," and to do so before our first, or next, heart attack or the traumatic sudden death of a friend or loved one with whom we regret not spending more time, or we develop an addiction, affliction, or dis-ease that is a signpost screaming, "I am not a dancing bear! I do not want to be a cog in the wheel of capitalism! I am sick and tired of working hard so that other people can get richer! I am fed up with people exploiting my limited time on planet Earth!"

The average retiree in America watches television forty-five hours a week. Are we working harder and harder just so we can spend the last twenty years of our lives on a sofa? I think we need a new metric for mental health, happiness, and success. And it could be different for every person. But if we buy into the current version of the supposed American dream, then we are signing up to live financially beyond our means, to be on hamster wheels of consumption, to constantly work until we drop dead or retire or are put out to pasture to make room for younger, hungrier workers.

If I am right and the current barometer of mental well-being relates to showing up for our jobs, to being productive members of society in order to earn money to pay our credit card debts, mortgages, and student loans, then instead of over 20 million Americans taking antidepressants every day, maybe it is time to reframe the American dream; build vibrant, loving, noncompetitive communities; take vacations; and allow time for people to bond with and attach to their families and friends. Maybe it is also time to stop blaming people and labeling people as lazy if they are not rich, stop ostracizing people who do not play the game of consumerism, and allow people to decide for themselves who they want to be and to find for themselves the things that will keep them at the higher ends of their happiness spectrums.

I devoted chapters 4 and 5 to romance and work because I believe that (if our health and safety are intact) many of the thousands of thoughts that rise to consciousness every day are greatly influenced by these two pillars of our society. These two pillars, work and romance, were firmly implanted in our minds during childhood through the fairy tales we learned, the songs we heard, the books we read, and the films and television shows we watched. Dreams of competing in the Olympics, of becoming professional athletes or musicians, famous actors or artists, or wealthy entrepreneurs are deeply rooted in our society. All of us have a limited time on earth, so I am asking you to question whether trying to attain someone else's goals or playing by someone else's rules regarding romance and competitive capitalism is bringing you peace and love and allowing you to be authentic. Or is consciously and subconsciously trying to please other people stressing you out?

In chapter 6 we examine how we temporarily escape the pressures of romance and business with sundry activities that are built into our society.

Chapter 6

How to Blow Off Steam and Keep Your Life Manageable

I can resist everything except temptation.
— OSCAR WILDE

Thirty years ago, while studying with Philip Rieff at the University of Pennsylvania, I became fascinated by Rieff's concept of remissions. Rieff taught that the mores, customs, ethics, and laws of Western culture were rooted in the Judeo-Christian sacred order. Although Thomas Jefferson advocated a "wall of separation between church and state" in America, we can see that our legal system and its interdicts are not estranged from the Ten Commandments. In particular, if we look at key issues during election cycles we observe divisions between religious and secular voters; for example, in the debate surrounding the legality of abortion in America, we can see that Christianity continues to influence our legal system.

In Western civilization, our morality is essentially Judeo-Christian — although we could also argue that some pagan rituals, too, pop up now and again. We are all familiar with the concept of transgression: if we transgress a law and are caught, then there is punishment, such as a fine, community service, or jail time. Sometimes we are made to spend time solitarily confined so that we can meditate more intensely on our crimes, and some transgressions in America, as you know — treason and murder — can be punishable by death. However, in contrast to its responses to the clearly delineated list of prohibited acts, such as murder, rape, and theft, each culture also builds in an approach to *somewhat forbidden yet ultimately forgivable* or at least ignored offenses that allow people to indulge in guilty pleasures and receive a slap on the wrist or a frown, rather than an electric chair: these guilty pleasures are what Rieff called remissive acts or remissions.

To describe remissions, I like to use the analogy of a pot of boiling water blowing off steam lest it blow its lid. Remissions are not as straightforward as transgressions, and in modern society personal boundaries often test what constitutes a remission in individual cases. For example, binge eating, online gambling, fourteen-hour video-game or cable-series marathons — maybe even some light bondage — may not make a blip on another person's remission radar. Recall that children rebel and individuate in different ways — some may bite the nipple that feeds them, while others may get tattoos or cut themselves — but my understanding is that whatever is declared illicit becomes titillating, enticing; and I agree with Freud that whatever is repressed returns sometime later even stronger. The goal of psychoanalysis (but not psychotherapy) is to excavate one's subconscious to understand how we developed our repressions and to release some of the negative emotions around them, such as shame, guilt, fear, anger, frustration, disappointment, sadness. I also appreciate Freud's notion of sublimation. Pent-up energy — mostly sexual — must be sublimated, and that sublimated energy is capable of producing, and is responsible for, art, literature, music, architecture, and so on. Camille Paglia offered a provocative opinion on sublimation when she wrote, "There is no female Mozart because there is no female Jack the Ripper," echoing Nietzsche's claim that men produce art as well as war because they are the "sterile animal," meaning that they cannot physically produce babies.

I am not asking you to agree or disagree; I am merely asking you to try on a new lens to analyze the society in which you were raised. Perhaps also recall how you were taught as an infant not to play with your tickle-spot in public, to eat food rather than throw it, not to punch or kick other humans — particularly siblings — not to run into traffic, not to lick the electric socket, not to throw your toys down the hill, not to drown your dolls, and so on. As a child, did you possibly have a double life in which you mischievously stayed up late hidden under the covers playing in a fantasy parallel universe or on another planet?

Did you...

- stay out past your assigned curfew?
- set something afire to see what would happen?
- do something unspeakable with or to food?
- urinate someplace you were told not to?
- act out in other weird ways because the interdicts seemed arbitrary and nonsensical to your unformed brain?

And now that you are an adult, do you not still have some sort of double life, do you not still commit an occasional peccadillo? For instance, do you sometimes find yourself...

- raiding the fridge and cupboards at 3:30 AM?
- downing a bottle of wine in front of the television?

- watching pornography at your desk or in your study when you are supposed to be working?
- shopping online at the office?
- checking a dating website even though you are not single?
- enjoying an occasional cigarette?
- spending Sundays from 10 AM to 10 PM at the pub drinking beer and watching sports?
- flooring your automobile just to see how fast you can go?
- taking two Ambien or Xanax when the doctor clearly told you to take only one?
- doing other activities that you really know you should not do but cannot help doing?

Those times when your mind says, "Fuck it!" or "Fuck it! Nobody tells me what to do! I am having another drink / piece of cake / Xanax! I deserve it!" Those are remissions. Maybe a lovely wooden coat hanger, or a towel, or an unwrapped bar of soap is mysteriously liberated from the hotel and placed in your luggage, and you justify or rationalize it in some way so that it is not actually stealing. Technically it is…hmm… stealing. But really, it is viewed as a remission in our culture. When hotels start implanting security chips in towels, hangers, and soap, well-dressed people who pay five hundred to three thousand dollars a night for suites are going to come up with better narratives than all the bestsellers in the world when their luggage starts setting off alarms. There is a reason why TVs, blow-dryers, radios, and other valuables are now nailed down in hotel rooms. Talk to hotel security personnel and ask them what percentage of the same hangers and towels will remain in their hotel after one year. Ask them how many blankets and televisions go missing year after year. This is why it is so interesting to study human consciousness. "Laws were made to be broken." "Power corrupts." Clichés are clichés because they are true.

Human beings enjoy testing boundaries. Think of all the classic comedies you love: many of the jokes revolve around people gently testing the norms of propriety and then being slapped on the wrist and forgiven or given another chance after demonstrating a modicum of shame and remorse. Think Groucho Marx. Think John Belushi in *Animal House* and *Blues Brothers*, Chevy Chase in *Fletch* and *Vacation*, Zach Galifianakis in *The Hangover* films, Larry David in *Curb Your Enthusiasm*. Think Marc Maron, John Oliver, Stephen Colbert, Chelsea Handler, Jimmy Kimmel, Dave Chappelle, and Conan O'Brien asking marginally inappropriate, provocative, or revealing questions while interviewing guests and pretending to have normal unscripted conversations. Asking someone on television the craziest place he or she ever made whoopee was shocking in the 1970s; now it is de rigueur. *If I went into the supermarket and asked the cashier some of the questions Chelsea Handler asks guests on her talk show, I would be arrested.* She is inappropriate to the point of catharsis so that we do not have to be.

I actually describe some people's behavior as the result of what I call "Chelsea Handler syndrome": the ability to make people feel extremely uncomfortable while remaining oblivious to the fact that you caused it. Yes, she does this under the guise of "being authentic" and is (1) not dumb and (2) often hysterical, particularly in her writing. All this proves is that authenticity does not bring out the best in everyone. Chelsea Handler is authentic (supposedly) to the point of being offensive. Brilliantly offensive. I have never met a happy comedian, but I believe that the ability to find humor in the absurdity of the things that we take to be "normal" is quite a gift.

Being constrained by a civilization's laws and regulations, combined with a low tolerance for emotional expression, produces discontents for some if not all of that civilization's inhabitants. Underneath our fashionable veneers we are still animals, and some of us happen to be more moody, rebellious, angry, predatory, ferocious — and less domesticated — than others. As a result, individuals pay a price for the privilege of social order, safety, security — for the freedom to stay out of continual fight-or-flight mode, for the fact that lions and tigers and other predators are not lurking in the bushes waiting to pounce on us. Although marauding gangs still plague some recesses of America, we live in a relatively safe country and enjoy more peace than most other civilizations, if I am not mistaken.

Remissions allow us occasional emotional and psychological releases from the constraints and constrictions of society. Celebrations such as parades and fraternity parties, football games in packed stadiums of sixty thousand revelers, soccer games, hockey games that sometimes spill over into the seats, violent video games, pornography, all allow people to feel things that most of us are prohibited from feeling during our normal work weeks. If we all acted like drunken, raucous football fans all the time, then there would be complete disorder, chaos, anarchy. But visit a sports bar on Sunday afternoon or Monday evening, or a heavy metal or hard rock concert, or Burning Man, or a rave or ecstatic dance party, and watch normally civilized adults release heightened emotions that would not go over well in offices or at most jobs, at Starbucks, at the mall, or in other public places.

Our society has a relatively narrow bandwidth of tolerated

emotions: in particular, we do not feel comfortable around angry women or sad men. If a woman were to stand on a street corner in a major metropolis angrily cursing or screaming, fairly soon someone would call the police to come examine her. And if the police thought she was disrupting the normally peaceful social order, they would call a short bus to give her a mandatory three-to-four-day vacation in a psychiatric ward to allow her to unwind and reconsider. If a man were to curl up in a ball weeping hysterically on a corner in a major metropolis, fairly soon someone would call the police to come examine him. And if the police thought he was disrupting the normally peaceful social order, they would call a short bus to give him a mandatory three-to-four-day vacation in a psychiatric ward to allow him time to "buck up," "be a man," and "get over" his grief. Nobody would really care if the man or woman had experienced a terrible tragedy that morning. We simply do not feel comfortable around angry women and sad men emoting in public places.

When interdicts are too rigid and not enough remissions are tacitly built into the system — when political regimes and governments are too repressive — then people rebel and riot until the authority releases its grip. Philip Rieff writes, "A remission too severely constrained becomes a decivilizing interdict, whereas one too broadly granted becomes an uncivilizing transgression." There is a razor's edge that most of us unwittingly walk. Has a close friend ever admitted a shocking double life to you? For example, has a friend ever told you he is the well-respected CEO of a billion-dollar corporation but occasionally enjoys cross-dressing with a dominatrix and indulging in fetishes that are not betrayed during board meetings by his four-thousand-dollar suit? Or has a friend ever admitted that she shoplifts items like lipstick that she can easily afford?

If you are not offended by the application of ancient philosophy to modern video games or cage fights, we can discuss Plato and Aristotle's debate: Plato thought that art and entertainment were mimetic; Aristotle thought art and entertainment were cathartic. Plato believed that if people saw violence they would imitate it; Aristotle believed that viewers would vicariously live that violence or sadness and, just by observing it, be less prone to act it out. The jury is still out on this. James Holmes dressed as "the Joker" and murdered twelve people during a Batman film; bar fights during football games supply evidence for Plato's case; millions of people playing violent video games or watching professional wrestling and not abusing their partners or pets lend credence to Aristotle's case. The point is that our society has interdicts against citizens committing acts of violence and sex publicly; yet if we turn on the television or computer or go to the movies we see little else. This is not good or bad any more than an iPhone in itself is inherently good or bad. But if everyone checked his or her iPhone all the time, there would be social disorder, chaos — car crashes, plane crashes, pedestrian accidents, and so on. We need rules and laws in order to coexist. But when rules and laws become too repressive, people revolt. Does the Sturm und Drang we view in film, at the theater, and on television — cage fights, boxing matches, and mixed martial arts competitions — allow us cathartically to feel emotions we are not allowed to express in polite society? Or does it cause some people to imitate bad behavior that they would otherwise be unfamiliar with?

Most remissions are things that we would consider relatively "normal" — some minor binge eating while on vacation, shopping intensely on Black Friday, gambling until the wee hours of the morning or visiting a strip club while in Las Vegas, extreme sports, video games, and so on. What I am interested in examining is how prohibitions and remissions affect the way we think and the way we interact with others daily. Let's say someone leads a double life: can he or she keep the secret half permanently separate from the public half? Which "life" or "self" would he or she consider to be more authentic? Or does embracing our shadow side, or dark tendency — as opposed to rejecting it — lead to a new type of holistic authenticity? In other cultures, light and dark, yin and yang, are two sides of the same coin. Everyone has a dark, or shadow, side, I believe. So the question is: Should we repress and shun our shadow or embrace it? Should we feel guilty about it and flagellate ourselves? Does it help if we are ashamed by our remissions (or does it only make them more titillating)? Is deeming these thoughts to be evil counterproductive? What if we learned how to embrace our shadow side and figure out harmless ways of exorcising these supposed demons?

In the television series *Billions*, the first scene of the first episode displays Paul Giamatti's character bound and being burned with a cigarette while he banters with his dominatrix. Finally she asks if she should urinate into the cigarette burn and he consents. She pees on his chest. We then see him eating breakfast with his wife and children and working that day as a prominent district attorney. In the last scene of the first episode, we realize that the dominatrix is really his loving wife, who is an extremely successful psychologist for a billion-dollar investment bank. These married urban parents have carved out a space for remissions so that the remissions do not interfere with their seemingly normal and average urban family life or their prestigious careers and accompanying social status. I am not implying that any of us would benefit from being tied up, burned, and urinated on. But it is fascinating that a prime-time television program portrays this new "normal" in family life in America.

As demonstrated by *Billions*, there is a whole range of sexual activities that are neither generally condoned nor condemned — some people enjoy them and some people think they are disgusting (and some people think they are disgusting and partake in them), some communities embrace them and some communities ostracize the people who engage in them. In some states various sexual practices may be illegal but seldom prosecuted — pornography, sodomy, stripping, prostitution, orgies, adultery, bigamy, public masturbation. Fourteen states still outlaw anal sex between two consenting men and refer to it in various documents as "deviant sexual conduct," "the infamous crime against nature," "sodomy," and "buggery." The court case *Lawrence v. Texas* rendered state's laws against sodomy essentially unenforceable, but it is interesting to live in a country in which homosexuals can marry but cannot legally have sex in some places.

Similarly, many people eat a whole range of intoxicating gustatory delights and desserts — chocolate, cakes, pies, cookies, ice cream, candies, gum, other sweets — but feel small twangs of guilt when doing so excessively. I see sugar and wheat, as well as salt, as minor remissions, particularly if our cardiologist has told us to avoid them.

I have worked with many patients who seem to briefly, mindlessly, indulge in some of these activities and treats as respites or distractions from their jobs, and sometimes as rewards for a job well done or even doing a job at all. I also know people who enjoy a cigarette and/or a glass of wine at the end of the workday as a ritual signifying that the workday is over. We are seemingly free to indulge in many activities that may or may not benefit our physical health but that appear to benefit our sanity in some intangible or undefinable way. Why else would we overeat, overdrink, or anesthetize or distract ourselves with hours and days of television, games, narcotics, and so on?

Jumping back to Aristotle, it seems as if the real issue in our society concerns moderation. Some people fail to understand the concept of diminishing returns. When some Americans hear that French people on average drink one glass of wine per day and live longer, they assume that if one glass per day is good for our health then two glasses must be better. And this is the type of circumstance where remissions tumble into afflictions and then addictions. As I mentioned in chapter 3, anyone who has worked a twelve-step program knows that addictions relate to resentments, which are usually uncovered in the fourth step, when the addict makes "a searching and fearless moral inventory" of himself. And I believe that most other transformational, educational, and personal-growth seminars and workshops — such as those on the Hoffman Process, Emotional Freedom Techniques, Kabbalah, and primal therapy, or those offered by Landmark and Tony Robbins — also teach that our minds create resentment when we want things that we cannot change to be different. Overcoming resentment entails:

- learning how to forgive others.
- learning how to forgive ourselves.
- learning to accept who we are.
- learning to accept our lives.
- being grateful for whatever privileges, freedoms, and gifts we enjoy.

- taking responsibility for and cleaning up whatever messes we have made.
- learning how to be of service to others (preferably while releasing our expectation of reciprocation).

All of these are tools designed to help us overcome the resentments (quite often about our supposedly imperfect childhoods) that often result in self-sabotage and self-harm.

Another part of the solution is discipline, which correlates with self-worth. If we do not have the discipline to abstain from a second or third drink or make commitments to regular healthy practices such as yoga, meditation, hiking, swimming, and so on, then there is probably an underlying self-worth issue. If we find the voice in our head saying, "What does it matter if I do a bong hit on Saturday morning?" then we probably resent something about our lives that makes us rebel against everything, including our own well-being.

I was once in a workshop where a Lebanese man in his twenties told the following story: "When I was a senior in high school, I cut my physics class most of the first part of the year. My physics teacher, too, was Lebanese, and he took me aside and said, 'Why are you busting my balls? You are just going to work in your father's shop when you graduate, so you do not need to take physics. Do us both a favor and drop my class. Okay?' I redoubled my efforts and passed physics, then went to college, and then I opened my own shop." The workshop leader casually asked the Lebanese guy: "What's the name of your shop?" "Bob's Shop," the man responded. The workshop leader repeated himself, saying, "No, it's not. What's the name of your shop?" The Lebanese guy was bewildered and guffawed: "My name is Bob. The name of my shop is Bob's Shop." "No, it's not," repeated the leader. "I am telling you," said the guy angrily, "the name of my shop is Bob's Shop, for God's sake!!" To which the leader replied, "The name of your shop is: *Not My Father's Shop.*"

As I said earlier, we emulate the characteristics of the caregivers we had when we were young as a way to retroactively subconsciously gain their approval and love; and we also subconsciously incarnate the opposite characteristics of the caregivers we had when we were young as a way to individuate from them. Becoming something in order to gain approval is inauthentic; being reactive and rebelling against something is also inauthentic. So when the child of hippies becomes a conservative, or the child of conservatives becomes a hippie, it does not mean this person decided who she wants to be. It means she decided who she *doesn't* want to be. That is why learning to be as authentic as possible — which may include embracing our shadow side, double life, and other tools we developed in order to individuate — is crucial to our own well-being.

Reacting against authority — via tattoos, self-harm such as cutting as an expression of agency/autonomy, binge drinking into obliviousness, and so on — often results in self-harm, which is why much of the rest of this book is devoted to helping you decide who you want to be and what life you wish to live, and to giving you tools to accomplish your goals. Many of us have not taken the time to consciously decide who we want to be and what lives we want to live, and have become who we are by default. Which is okay if we are 100 percent happy and truly believe that our lives have been and are perfect in every way possible. Otherwise it is time for us to learn how to own our lives, how to be proactive about who we are and what we will do during our brief time on earth. And then we will be able to consciously create balanced lives full of the love and intimacy we need in order to heal the wounds we have, clean up our resentment, and engage in activities that keep us at the higher end of our happiness ranges.

We must become mindful of our remissions and do everything in our power to create balanced lives that include blowing off steam in positive ways, such as yoga, hiking, swimming, meditation, communing with friends and loved ones, and so on. And I am not against martial arts, watching violent sports in moderation, drinking in moderation, or smoking in moderation, among other things. However, when we make assumptions about "why" we choose particular remissions, then our minds may trick us by saying, "Fuck it! Have another drink, have another toke, shoplifting is exciting, speeding is cool, take another Xanax, watch a few more episodes of that series! Porn is a victimless crime! Go ahead! What difference does it make? Who's gonna know? Who's gonna care? Fuck it! Just do it! Fuck it!" When that happens, our remissions quickly devolve into afflictions and then into life-impeding addictions. Once an addiction takes hold, only a massive shift in personal identity can overcome that addiction. We need new narratives. And it is not easy. If you have ever watched an addict struggle and relapse, then you know what I am talking about. The tools I propose offer a preemptive strike against addiction. If you are already in the throes of an addiction, then you need to find a rehabilitation system that resonates with you. I often recommend Noah Levine's *Refuge Recovery* to those who cannot subscribe to the theism of the twelve-step program. I am unaware of other rehabilitation programs that are as successful as Refuge Recovery and the Anonymous twelve-step programs.

Remissions are what they are. They are not inherently good or bad in themselves. They are integral components to maintaining social order. And yet if they become afflictions or addictions — if our lives become "unmanageable" and we are unable to regulate our emotions to fit the bandwidth of tolerability that our society demands, and if we do not have the discipline to lead a balanced, more or less harmonious life — then it is time for a rethink. Maybe it will help us consciously decide who we want to be and how we want to live, and help us proactively choose activities that will keep us in the higher range of our happiness spectrums. When you finish this chapter please take five to ten minutes to write down:

- who you want to be.
- what type of life you want to live.
- what activities will help you lead that life.
- what activities will inhibit you from leading that life.
- your addictions.
- your remissions.

Left to their own devices our minds run amok, awry, and aground. We must be proactive about our thinking if we want to be happy. Indifference is a cop-out. I have heard fellow teachers try to justify indifference as the Buddhist understanding of nonattachment, which is lovely if you live alone in a cave high on a mountain and people leave you enough food to survive. Then there is no harm in mistaking indifference for awakening. But those of us who seek personal equanimity and inner peace within Western civilization must try to be congruent — mitigate hypocrisy and have our outer worlds match our inner worlds. Hypocrisy is a surefire path to misery. Do you remember Republican senator Larry Craig, who railed against homosexuality and was later arrested in the men's restroom in an airport for soliciting gay sex? Examples of this type of hypocrisy abound in our culture.

What I am saying is that behavior and the intentions behind it do not manifest ex nihilo. I think a wave of honesty is emerging regarding remissions such as the sexual play shown in *Billions* or *Eyes Wide Shut*, dancing all night at Burning Man or a rave, and the intense screaming and sweating in the first few rows of rock concerts. Intentionally creating frames (specific places and times) to let loose and blow off some steam is extremely helpful to maintaining social order — *lest the pot boil over.*

Congruence is the opposite of hypocrisy. Incongruence is difficult to reconcile both internally and externally. We need to learn how to proactively surf obvious paradoxes such as "I know that politics today is mostly theatrical bullshit, but I still have to do everything in my power to make a difference." A part of being at ease and having peace of mind is understanding that our society and our life situations — including our socioeconomic levels, attachment styles, remissions, schools, sex roles, gender roles, friendships — are like the oceans that fish swim in. Unless we are able to gain insight into things that most fish take for granted — namely, capitalism (the way our culture propagates busyness and abhors idleness), religion, and science — then we are really just swimming blindly and should not be surprised if we run aground, end up beached.

Do you think anyone in Salem said, "Y'know, I'm not 100 percent certain that burning these witches is going to solve our problems"? Do you think anyone told a feudal lord, "Y'know, someday there won't be lords and serfs. Someday there will be factories, and laborers will earn paper money...and in about five hundred years the most amazing invention of all will double the average life span in just one generation: it will be called a *toilet*." None of us can see the future or the future paradigm. Personally, I hope it is one of compassion rather than competition, but the human race really only shifts en masse because of bangs, not whimpers. Our ocean of highly competitive, consumer-based capitalism mixed with science and religion is extremely myopic. It results in our country coming up thirteenth among all nations on a happiness scale. We need to stop considering things to be normal just because they exist. If you watch television and films, dysfunctional relationships are normal. Millennials, in particular, often learn what they know about love and affection from pop culture and pornography — if that is not depressing then I do not know what is! Einstein said the level of consciousness that created a problem will be unable to fix it. Isn't it time we started raising our consciousness and learn to understand the matrices that gave rise to our problems?

Specifically, we need to learn how to take ourselves off autopilot, take ourselves off the hedonic treadmills that our minds place us on, and decide for ourselves what will let us be happy and lead meaningful lives. There is no chance for equanimity if we either allow other people to decide who we are, or simply react against those we do not want to be like. We need to figure out our paths for ourselves. As Proust wrote, "We do not receive wisdom; we must discover it for ourselves after a journey that no one can take for us or spare us." Maybe tai chi and hiking will give you insight into who you authentically are and what parts of your way of being you should keep or shed. For me it was making commitments to regular yoga and meditation practices and cultivating my sense of wonder, which meant traveling; it meant going back and reading classic texts; going to at least one museum each month, one movie each week, and symphony and jazz concerts whenever possible; it meant studying consciousness and philosophy; reading biographies and autobiographies of all the artists, musicians, writers, filmmakers, and philosophers whose work moved me; learning to embrace my shadow side; being open to various explorations of consciousness; and intentionally carving out limited space and time for my remissions. These are the activities and practices that have helped me continue to learn, grow, and evolve.

Beginning in the next chapter, we will explore what fills your heart and soul with bliss, what is your true calling. Chapters 1 through 6 of this book have been intended to raise questions regarding authenticity. I am asking you to examine your own comfort zone, your understanding of yourself, to deconstruct your personal identity and start developing new narratives, to strive to be as authentic as possible given the series of nested cages that we are trapped in — namely, our society's laws and regulations, its low tolerance for emotions, our own attachment styles, the resentments that the mind creates, the way we grieve losses, our way of being in the world, gender roles, money, ownership, friendships, media, and so on. The irony in writing a book about authenticity and exploring whether authenticity is even remotely possible is not lost on me. I find that the truth often lies in paradoxes. Language is both a cage and infinite. "I could be bounded in a nutshell and count myself a king of infinite space," says Hamlet to Rosencrantz and Guildenstern.

Now that you have deconstructed your self, let's spend the rest of the book employing tools to figure out and reconstruct, as authentically as possible, who you want to be and what tools to employ to be that person. Let's talk about authenticity in terms of congruence, in terms of presence and being present, in terms of genuinely connecting with other people, of learning your vocation or true calling, of listening to messages from the higher power of your understanding, and of leaving positive footprints on Mother Earth.

Chapter 7

What Are You Doing on Planet Earth?

Let's reflect on whatever part of us is able to observe our thoughts. All of us have been around pets and other animals who simply exhibit "doingness" — playing when they feel playful, sleeping when they feel tired, defecating when their bodies need to defecate. They don't need to think about or plan their lives very far in advance. Aside from responding to the natural rhythms of the day and the seasons, undomesticated animals do not consciously put themselves on a daily schedule. Nor do they appear to tell elaborate stories about their pasts or imagine their futures. I am willing to bet they also do not ponder their own mortality and possible future suffering. The ability to conceive of our own nonexistence while we exist, and to imagine the various ways we might die, is apparently exclusive to human consciousness.

Before we explore Advaita Vedanta, let's arbitrarily categorize human consciousness in terms of levels:

- Level 1 is "doing," or "doingness" or "doing, without thinking about what we are doing": "being in the zone" and not second-guessing ourselves — the way animals act.

- Level 2 is "thinking about what we are doing before, during, and after we do it": having thoughts
about our activities rise to consciousness, such as
"Oh, I am walking now…" "I have to wash clothing later…"
- Level 3 is "thinking about thinking": being able to
observe our thoughts without actually acting upon
them.
- Level 4 is "thinking abstractly": being able to
cogitate about things such as laws of quantum me-
chanics, calculus, and so on.

I love all meditations and relaxation exercises that guide
us to observe our thoughts, because when we learn how to
watch our thoughts float through our mindscreens like clouds
passing through the sky or leaves floating down a river, we
can gain insights into their absurdly repetitive and irrationally
negative nature. In other types of meditations, we can learn
to categorize our thoughts according to whether they concern
the past, present, or future, and whether they are positively or
negatively charged or neutral. Or we can watch the segues between thoughts and how parts of them morph and stream into
others. Also we can make a distinction between discernment
and judgment. An example of discernment is: "Look both ways
before crossing the street." A judgment occurs when our mind
extrapolates, overgeneralizes, and tells us: "Cars are bad (because they can hit you and harm or kill you)." As noted earlier,
I believe that the primary function of the mind is to keep us
alive and stave off future traumas. The mind creates loads of
judgments and prejudices in its attempts to keep us safe. Guess
what? They work! If you are prejudiced against roaring wild-
fires, exploding cars, loaded unlocked machine guns, oceans,

landslides, high places without guardrails, flying airplanes, and swords, that is because being around them exponentially increases your chance of being harmed or killed.

One of my goals in writing this book is to bring some of our subconscious beliefs or assumptions to consciousness, so that we can get some insight into our ways of being in the world, how we choose to present ourselves to others, and our attachment styles. This will help us make healthier decisions when we debate whether to lean in or avoid something. It will also help us realize how prejudices and fears built during childhood may influence our adult decisions, and how to choose healthier remissions to blow off steam.

Chapters 7 and 8 are the perfect place to examine two eastern philosophies — Advaita Vedanta and Mahayana Buddhism — to see if either can shed light on our predicaments, lend fresh perspectives on consciousness, and help us see reality more clearly. I will not be proselytizing. I actually believe that, on the whole, religion has done more harm than good — crusades, wars, prejudices, racism, oppression, and so on — mainly owing to the fact that most religions are dogmatic and promote that their way of seeing the world is the best for everyone. People should be free to believe whatever they believe as long as those beliefs do not affect other people. Unfortunately, if you look at the history of religions, there is really a great deal of unnecessary squabbling, fighting, nailing people to crosses, burning people alive, beheading people, quartering people, sacrifices, flagellations — on the whole, a grand tradition of unpleasantness. On the other hand, contemplating philosophy has rarely led to heinous destruction of human life. We shall be looking, then, at philosophies regarding consciousness; or more precisely, we will be examining Hindu eschatology and Buddhist psychology.

Just as Christianity has many denominations — Protestant, Lutheran, Calvinist, Pentecostal, Quaker, Unitarian, and so on — Hinduism has six *darshanas* (viewpoints or schools). There is Samkhya, Yoga (as a philosophy; not the physical asana practice that we do in yoga studios and gyms throughout America), Nyaya, Dvaita Vedanta, Vishishtadvaita Vedanta, and Advaita Vedanta. However, all of the schools deal with the following questions:

- What is the nature of the divine?
- What is the nature of the individual soul?
- How was the world created?
- How do we attain freedom/liberation/joy?

Some of the *darshanas* have ornate cosmologies, myths, and gods, and most of them emphasize different understandings of the divine and how the universe was created. But for the purposes of this book, let's examine the philosophy of the *darshana* of Advaita Vedanta. For me, Advaita Vedanta is the root of the modern practices of yoga and meditation that are becoming more and more popular in our culture. To understand the philosophy of Advaita Vedanta, we need to be familiar with three main concepts:

Brahman: "That without attributes" is the best translation I have heard for the Sanskrit word *Brahman*. If you can think of a thing or about it, it is *not* Brahman. One way to imagine it is as an imperceptible matrix or field that connects all particles in the universe, where there is no such thing as time, and where infinite realities intersect, as portrayed in films such as

Interstellar. Within our culture, the word *G-d* is often written with a dash or hyphen to express the fact that the nature of God is ineffable, infinite, beyond any human language, too vast to put into words — attempting to do so would be like trying to photograph the entire clear blue infinite sky. If I asked you to close your eyes and imagine the infinite, you would probably revisit images of constellations or skies that you had seen during your life. These images are known as "placeholders." We cannot imagine the infinite. It is "what we do not know that we do not know" multiplied by a million. Poetry, music, and painting can point to the infinite, we can get glimpses of it or tastes of it through meditation and yoga, but experiences of the infinite usually overwhelm our minds. A nice metaphor is that we are drops of water in the ocean of Brahman. Imagine being one drop of water in the middle of the Pacific or Atlantic: it is overwhelming — is it not?

Atman: We can translate the Sanskrit word *Atman* as our Higher Self or soul. I don't know your religious beliefs, but unless you are what Gore Vidal calls a "born-again atheist," then you have probably entertained the possibility that we are more than just flesh and bones, that there is something spiritual or energetic about us. I mean, the chances of the chromosomes of your father meeting with the chromosomes of your mother and creating you are a trillion to one.

Maya: The best way to think about maya is as everything we perceive through our five senses — all of our perceptions, all of the sensations we receive through our senses and process through our minds are ephemeral, not permanent. They are mutable, changing, and changeable. That is maya — perceptual, phenomenal reality.

The word *Vedanta* simply means "the end of the Vedas" — the end of the Vedic period — which is when things began to be written down; the Vedas had been transmitted only orally for thousands of years. Just as the Talmud is commentary on the Torah, the Upanishads are commentaries on the Vedas. The Upanishads are the texts of Vedanta, the stories and poems and philosophies written over hundreds of years by anonymous authors who wrestled with and tried their best to point to understandings of the ineffable divine, or absolute.

There is a paradox in trying to use language to discuss something that is paralinguistic, beyond words, but that is what the Upanishads do. One of the classic phrases is *Neti neti*, which means that the divine is "not this, not that." It is "without attributes," so there is no way to conceive it and no way to intelligently discuss it. *Neti neti* indicates that Brahman is not going to be anything we can think. If we are thinking about something — say, placeholders for the infinite as in paintings of interdimensional matrices by Alex Grey or monoliths by Mark Rothko — it is not actually Brahman. Another popular phrase from the Upanishads is *Tat tvam asi*, which translates into "Thou art That" or "I am That" or "Thou art G-d" or some "That" indicating that our Atman is buried deep beneath the maya of our mind but that it is our true essence. Yoga and meditation are tools to help us temporarily transcend maya and realize the nonduality, the oneness of Atman and Brahman.

The Vedas function in a manner similar to that of our Judeo-Christian Bible, although there are no firm dates for either the Vedas or the Upanishads. Some scholars date the Vedas to as far back as 5000 BCE and the Upanishads to sometime around 1000 BCE. The Upanishads were codified into a philosophy by Sankara around the eighth century CE. *Advaita* means "nondual," so what we perceive as dualism or dualistic is illusory. Using the three terms above — *Brahman, Atman,* and *maya* — is how we can understand Advaita Vedanta or nondualism: everything that we perceive through our five senses, and that the mind translates into language and stories — all thoughts, feelings and perceptions (maya) — is ephemeral, passing, changing, and changeable. (Most of the time the words *illusory* or *illusion* are used to describe maya, but I am avoiding them here because thoughts and feelings seem extremely real when they are occurring. So just think of maya as the stream of consciousness in the mind that relates to how thoughts rise to consciousness, please.)

Yoga and meditation are tools designed to help people (temporarily) transcend maya — to go to the other side of or beyond human consciousness, where we will realize that Atman and Brahman are nondual, are really one and the same. Maya — the hamster wheel of thinking — prevents us from realizing our divine essence and our interconnectedness with everyone and everything. The word *yoga* means "yoking" or "union." When we practice yoga we are transcending maya to realize the unity of Atman and Brahman; or we can express it proactively by saying that we are uniting our mind, spirit, and body with the divine (which is really already our true essence once we transcend maya).

I understand that these concepts may sound foreign, religious, and even cultish to some people who are unfamiliar with yoga and meditation, but for the purposes of this chapter I ask you to try on this philosophy as you would try on a blouse or shirt at your favorite store to see if it fits. And after we have tried on the concept of Atman, or soul, to see if it resonates with us, then I would like to explore four other Hindu concepts:

Karma: Karma is defined as the law of action and reaction. The notion of karma is pervasive even in Western culture. Whereas some people prefer to talk about "luck," which seemingly occurs at random, other people do not wish to believe there is no rhyme or reason for why things happen. So, we believe in karma. For example, we are driving in a crowded city and it appears we will arrive late to the symphony, and then a car magically pulls out of a parking spot directly in front of the concert hall (and maybe even leaves the meter paid for the next few hours!). Many people would say, "Wow...good parking karma!" We all understand the concept of karma, but if we truly believe in karma, that what happens in the universe is not 100 percent random and accidental, then that leads us logically to the concept of samsara.

Samsara: If you think about it, believing in karma but not reincarnation would be irrational, mostly because it is erroneous to say something like: "Oh, she cheated on her SATs when she was sixteen, so it is karma that her husband cheated on her." Karma would not and could not function like that. So the problem with believing in karma is that the events of one lifetime cannot be explained within the confines of one lifetime. Karma is actually extremely complex and beyond our ken, incalculable; but if we believe that some people have naturally good karma (and not just for finding parking spots), then it implies that we believe in samsara, because events cannot be explained within one lifetime. For example, a baby born with a deformity would obviously be the result of previously generated karma, which necessitates a belief in samsara, the wheel of reincarnation. Psychiatrist Ian Stevenson of the University of Virginia documented hundreds of cases of children who remembered their past lives. The majority of Americans do not believe in reincarnation, but many other cultures do believe in it. My personal theory is that there is an inverse correlation between language acquisition and remembrances of past lives, given that those memories are usually extinguished by the time children are eight or nine years old, according to Stevenson.

Again, if you do not already believe that human beings have souls, and that souls generate karma over lifetimes, then just for the purposes of this chapter please imagine that we do have souls and that they transmigrate over the course of multiple human lifetimes. I like how Hamlet phrases it in his letter to Ophelia, which Polonius reads to the king and queen: "Whilst this machine is to him, Hamlet." As opposed to imagining that we are bodies with souls, we can go one step further and try on the inverse: we can imagine ourselves as spiritual beings or souls temporarily inhabiting these human incarnations, or "borrowing" these fleshy "machines" — as Hamlet calls them — for our particular incarnations as "Ira," "Hamlet," "Alice," "Carol," and so on. If we believe in the concepts of karma and soul, then it should not be an intellectual stretch to entertain the possibility of reincarnation.

And if you are 100 percent certain that you are soul-free, that the universe is occurring completely at random and there is no such thing as karma, then I am probably not going to convince you of karma, souls, and reincarnation right now. However, I suggest that you spend some time researching the work of Dr. Stevenson and decide whether 100 percent of the cases of children with birthmarks that resemble the fatal wounds of their supposed previous incarnations are complete fictions. And if you do prefer to believe in fortunate and unfortunate luck, rather than good and bad karma, then you can skip ahead to chapter 8.

Moksha: So if you are on board for the concept of samsara, then you will also understand the concept of moksha. Moksha is liberation from the wheel of samsara. It means that we have burned off our negative karma from our previous lifetimes and do not need to evolve or learn any more. We are released from reincarnating and can just enjoy the rest of eternity in bliss instead of dealing with mundane problems that earthlings endure.

Dharma: Lastly, the most important and applicable part of Advaita Vedanta that we must explore is the concept of dharma. Reflect on the mandate of all schools of Hinduism: to determine the nature of the divine, of the individual soul, how the world was created, and how we attain freedom/liberation/ joy. What is the missing link that threads together Brahman, Atman, maya, karma, samsara, and moksha? It is dharma. On the macro level, dharma is the principle that orders the universe — it is how and why the universe is functioning, and the point of our universe and all of life in it. There are many theories provided in the luscious stories and fables of Hindu texts, but what is important here is what you believe. Do you prefer to live in a universe occurring at random, where artists and musicians like Mozart and Van Morrison write beautiful music because they are lucky? That Mozart's and Van Morrison's music is the result of random experiments of notes? (This is what Brian Eno believes, by the way.)

Or do you prefer to live in a universe where musicians and artists and poets "channel" or "receive" bits of music or images of paintings or poems and then transcribe them into languages that other people can appreciate? (This is what Elizabeth Gilbert believes is the creative process.) Because, although *dharma* on the macro level means "the principles that order the universe," on the micro, or individual, level, *dharma* means "how we relate to the ordered universe." In other words, what are our vocations? *Voco* in Latin best translates as "calling." But "callings" do not occur ex nihilo. If we have a calling or vocation, this means *something* is calling us — right? It implies that we are receiving some information from somewhere that points us in a particular direction.

Believing in dharma relates to basic existentialism: what are we doing on planet Earth? If we do not believe in dharma and we prefer to believe that the universe is occurring completely at random, then how or why do we know if we should be parents or doctors or painters or police officers or poets or scientists or musicians? Obviously we have tastes; we have discernment. Where do these come from? Genetics? Randomly? Joseph Campbell said, "Follow your bliss," which for me is the modern understanding of "Follow your dharma," the primary lesson of the Bhagavad Gita. If we listen closely — as we do when we practice yoga and meditation — we receive information in the form of likes and dislikes, we are "called" by our tastes to participate in certain activities and avoid others.

In psychologist Sonja Lyubomirsky's research on happiness, she found that people who have *jobs* — things one does solely to earn money, like dig graves, sweep streets, or flip burgers — are miserable. People who have *careers* — long-term jobs that they are not passionate about in, say, finance or law (where one gets caught in golden handcuffs, the type of thing I mentioned in chapter 5) — are also fairly miserable. But people who know their *vocations*, their callings, and who can somehow manage to earn their livings by doing what the universe is calling them to do, are happy. The lesson I take away from the classic Hindu story of Arjuna and Krishna in the Bhagavad

Gita is that Arjuna must follow his dharma, which on that day is calling him to be a warrior. Many people do not have a choice and must work at jobs they dislike in order to survive; but if we have a choice, then our top priority should be doing work that fulfills our heart and soul.

Similarly, there is a direct correlation between having a sense of wonder, being curious about life, and happiness. We must know what creative outlets feed our spirit, our soul, our heart, our passion, our Higher Self (for atheists I use "Mystery"). Do we love playing or listening to music? Do we love painting or admiring great artworks? Do we love nature and feeling united with the trees, plants, and earth? Do we love the water and feel at home swimming? Everyone has something that nourishes his or her inner self, or Higher Self — looking at the Grand Canyon, preparing sumptuous meals, running marathons, writing songs, reading books, helping others, and so on. It is our responsibility to learn what feeds our heart and spirit. And hopefully we can also earn our living from the activities that nourish us.

This is why having a philosophy behind our meditation and yoga practices is so important. Because when we get glimpses or tastes of the divine, moments of respite from the hamster wheel in our mind, gaps between thoughts, then we can equate whatever we consider to be the watcher of those thoughts with our Higher Self. And when we can tune in to our Higher Self, then we can discern our dharma. Even if it sounds airy-fairy or unscientific to you, maybe you can explore the possibility of mystery trumping science, the idea that there is order to the universe beyond human perception and science.

In the nineteenth century, Nietzsche suggested that our culture's faith in a Christian God would become a faith in science.

In the 1960s, Thomas Kuhn proposed that scientific paradigms shift every generation. Science has equations for calculating gravity, yet it cannot really explain why the ebb and flow of the tides correlate to the 29.5-day lunar cycle. There is no scientific "theory of everything" (yet), and I am not sure that Western science is even capable of accurately mapping the universe. Much that was considered normal three hundred to four hundred years ago is now considered absurd and unscientific. In three hundred to four hundred years, historians will look back on gasoline-fueled cars the way we look back on horse-drawn carriages; they will look back on our cement cities the same way we look back on cavemen. In 2400, people might say things like: "Those imbeciles... They had to use those silly devices called iPhones — they did not realize they could communicate telepathically." Or: "Hard to believe they had to use those silly things called airplanes — they did not realize they could teleport themselves."

If science is constantly shifting and people can find "scientific" studies (holding enough variables constant) to "prove" almost anything — "New studies prove that tobacco and high-fructose corn syrup are healthy and climate change is fake!" — then why do people have so much faith in it? (Hint: people fear uncertainty and would rather be wrong than say, "I am not sure" or "We do not know.") When people start sentences with phrases such as "Did you hear that *they* just discovered..." or "*They* just did a study and proved that...," I sometimes ask, "Who's 'they'?" I think that we all imagine this elusive "them" as a gaggle of scientists in lab coats at Harvard University with their hands on their chins like Rodin's *Thinker*. However, if you can see the forest through the trees, you will find that "science" is really just a temporary *consensus* on facts that we currently agree map various phenomena as accurately as possible for the time being. And both the reality out there (for example, changes in climate, sea levels, soil erosion, and so on) and our consensuses regarding those phenomena shift and evolve.

Returning to our own consciousness, whatever part of us is able to observe our thoughts is what we can think of as Atman, our Higher Self or soul. And if we espouse the philosophy of Advaita Vedanta, then through meditation, yoga, or other activities we can glimpse that peaceful place beyond our thoughts, we can realize that our soul is synonymous with Brahman, nirvana, G-d, Jesus, sunyata (the voidness or nothingness of Buddhism)...It actually does not matter what we call it (since no words can describe the ineffable anyway), as long as we recognize that our essential self *has* thoughts, and not that we are thoughts. Descartes put our culture on a misguided trajectory when he made thinking the premier attribute of existence. Instead of "I think therefore I am," it would be healthier for us to believe: "I breathe therefore I am" or "I observe therefore I am." Getting our personal identity through the hamster wheel in our head — through what we "do" and ruminating about it — is an accident looking for a place to happen.

And for those "born-again atheists" who are 100 percent sure that karma and dharma and souls and reincarnation are absolute fictions, we explore Buddhist psychology next, as a prescription for alleviating mental suffering.

Chapter 8

Can You Be a Buddhist If You're an Atheist?

For me, there is no such thing as Buddhism. And if there is something called Buddhism, then it is not a religion. Let me ask you: Do you think that Jesus Christ at any point during his abbreviated life said, "Hey, guys, do me a favor... from now on would you please call yourself *Christians?*" Do you think the Navajo and Cherokee and Sioux and Dakota and Apache elders got together (when they weren't busy fighting each other) 350 years ago and said, "Y'know, that Italian guy who never touched foot on our soil, Amerigo Vespucci? I heard that he's a decent fellow, and those dark-skinned people that we heard about — the ones with the nifty spices — on the other side of the planet in India, the place where Christopher Columbus was heading when he got waylaid? ... Our skin tone is probably about the same as theirs, so I think it would be easier for everyone if we just call ourselves 'American' (after Italian mapmaker Amerigo Vespucci) and 'Indians' (after the people on the other side of the planet who we have never seen) from now on and be done with it. Whatcha think? The whole Navajo-Cherokee-Sioux-Dakota-Apache thing is kinda confusing anyway. 'American Indians' makes sense — doesn't it"?

"Buddhism" is a concept that other people created in order to put a wide range of practices, tools, and techniques into one basket. Monks follow the Buddha's teachings and probably identify with traditions such as Theravada and Mahayana, and then with further subdivisions such as Pure Land, Zen, Nichiren, Vajrayana, and so on. More specifically, I do not believe that Buddhism is a religion — which means that nobody is going to ask us to convert from whatever religion with which we already affiliate. What we refer to as Buddhism is a prescription to alleviate suffering. *A prescription to alleviate suffering.* And it entails practices, tools, and techniques primarily designed to help alleviate human suffering — often simply by making us aware of the human mind's inherent tendency to cling to joyful or positive experiences and avert pain and other negative experiences. Very simple.

And as I mentioned in chapter 7, I love all meditations and relaxation exercises that guide us to observe our thoughts, because when we learn how to watch thoughts float across our mindscreens like clouds passing through the sky or like leaves floating down a river, then we can gain insights into the cause of our suffering. And if we can observe our thoughts and learn how to temporarily dis-identify with them, we get a respite from all the suffering they cause, in the manner the Buddha prescribed.

Siddhartha Gautama was born around 500 BCE. Just as Jesus was born into the Jewish faith, Siddhartha Gautama was born into the Hindu faith. He was a prince, and his father the king sequestered him so that he would not see pain, suffering, and death. Supposedly, when he was twenty-nine years old he left the castle and saw pain, suffering, and death. He then set out on a journey to ascertain the root causes of suffering. Finally he became "awakened" (the word *Buddha* means "awakened one"), and he came to the following conclusions, known as the Four Noble Truths and the Eightfold Path:

The Four Noble Truths

1. The essence of life (as perceived by our consciousness) is dukkha (suffering, anxiety, stress).
2. The root cause of dukkha is desire, which manifests as clinging or craving, and aversion.
3. It is possible to stop the suffering.
4. The way to stop the suffering is the Eightfold Path.

The Eightfold Path (with My Commentary)

A most propitious understanding of the nature of things: Everything is impermanent — we are impermanent, our thoughts are impermanent, and our emotional states are impermanent. The root cause of our suffering is the mind's desire to cling to impermanent positive (happy, joyful) states and stave off negative (unhappy, upsetting) states. As previously stated, I believe the mind's primary goal is to keep us alive and preclude potential future (unavoidable) pain. We can see the inherent paradox here, since we are all going to die and all going to experience pain while we are alive. *The craving to extend our ephemeral happy states and preclude unhappy states will always result in frustration and disappointment, because both are impossible.* As a result, having the most accurate view of reality possible — that we will all experience joys and sorrows, and that it is impossible to extend or deny them — is the way to alleviate suffering.

Most propitious intention: This tenet is the most important to me. I think of intention as akin to a beacon that guides a ship to shore. I believe human beings are rather myopic as a species and that we repress our own mortality until the last possible moment and then are surprised. In particular, it appears that many teenagers in our culture believe they are invincible and err on the side of recklessness. Once we realize that life is impermanent and our lives are finite, we find that having discipline and focus helps us accomplish more of the things we wish to accomplish, leading to more meaningful lives. Having intentions and accomplishing goals add meaning to our lives. But as I stated in chapter 3, in our culture *we are taught to desire the wrong things*; so even if we achieve or accomplish or obtain them, any happiness they bring is brief and often ultimately disappointing.

Deciding our intentions as adults is one of the keys of Buddhist psychology and will figure prominently in my discussion of congruence in chapter 10. Most of us were subconsciously taught — primarily through popular culture — that if we become wealthy, marry the ideal person, live the American dream of homeownership, fences, cars, mortgages as tax deductions, and children, we will be happy. Yet as I have pointed out, the things we learned as children to desire — including happiness itself — do not help us attain happiness. However, the Buddha discovered that having a beacon to guide us through life engenders happiness.

If we know that the one thing that correlates most strongly with happiness is the quality of our intimate relationships, how we connect with and attach to other people, then why is so much of our mental life devoted to things that do not bring us happiness, such as trying to earn more money and acquire more stuff? I honestly believe that if we wake up each morning and say to ourselves, "Whenever I die — today or in eighty years — I would like my tombstone to read 'Beloved,'" then that intention will guide us to make healthier decisions about our daily lives and relationships, it will inspire us to be kind to ourselves and to others, and it will help us avoid doing things that are incongruent with what we know is best for us.

You will notice above that I seem to have contradicted myself — this is one of the many problems that Americans have with Buddhist philosophy, including the doctrine of no-self or no permanent self: I said that we should desire reliable intimate relationships, desire having "Beloved" on our tombstones, desire discipline and intentions... and that the root of all suffering is desire. It could be argued that even not-desiring is a desire, so how did the Buddha skirt this paradox? *Through nonattachment.* I have had skeptics try to throw a monkey wrench into my engine in public classes by saying, "Well, if I did not have any desire, I would just sit in bed all day, masturbate, and eat licorice." Ironically one would still need desire to sit in bed, masturbate, and eat licorice. The point is not to eliminate *all* desire but to be conscious of our desires, to choose to practice the ones that benefit us most in the long term and not be attached to the outcomes.

Indifference is not enlightenment or awakening; indifference is a cop-out. If you live alone in a cave high on a mountain, then it is easy to mistake indifference to things like cold and hunger for awakening. In our society, awakening relates to congruence: having who we are match who we know we should be. Awakening is about proactively surfing obvious paradoxes, such as: "I know that politics today is bullshit, but I still have to do everything in my power to make the world a better place."

This is why we all need to learn how to take ourselves off autopilot, off the hedonic treadmill that the mind places us on, and decide for ourselves what will really make us happy and allow us to lead meaningful lives. There is no chance for equanimity if we allow other people to decide who we should be.

Most propitious speech: Avoiding harsh and senseless speech, refraining from verbal misdeeds such as lying, divisive speech, and gossip. Tabloid "news" — gossip about the lives of celebrities — has reached epic proportions in our culture. I argued in chapter 1 that language creates reality. Using words to gossip about fellow talented and flawed human beings can be distracting if not entirely wasteful. Words should be used to promote harmony. Slander, lying, harsh speech, and gossip do not engender affection. We do not appreciate when people slander us, lie to us, speak harshly to us, or gossip about us, so why would we spend time gossiping about others?

Most propitious action or conduct: Refraining from physical misdeeds such as killing, stealing, and sexual misconduct. As His Holiness the Dalai Lama states, "My religion is compassion." Compassion correlates more strongly with our innate interdependence than with the competition induced by our economic system; interdependence — being able to attach to, connect with, and rely on others — is the key correlate of happiness. Competition without compassion could lead to dishonesty, stealing, and killing. Nobody wants to live in such a world — choosing compassionate actions is always preferable to dissembling or taking advantage of others.

Most propitious livelihood: Avoiding trades that directly or indirectly harm others, such as selling slaves, weapons, intoxicants, or poisons. As stated in chapter 7 regarding jobs, careers, and vocations, choosing a healthy livelihood was important to the Buddha, too. He believed that earning a living in a harmless, peaceful, and compassionate manner helped prevent suffering.

Most propitious effort: Abandoning negative or unwholesome states of mind, preventing negative or unwholesome states that have yet to arise, and sustaining positive or wholesome states of mind. This precept is both simple and complicated, and I think we regard it the same way we think of remissions: we all experience negative and unwholesome thoughts. Instead of adding judgments such as "I am a bad person" or "I stink" and repressing those thoughts, it is less harmful in the long run if we learn to embrace our shadow sides and learn to sublimate and fit them into congruent narratives about ourselves. This is just my opinion, but I will argue in chapter 10 that congruence trumps hypocrisy. It bodes favorably for our long-term happiness if we are authentic about our thoughts and desires and make healthy decisions about them, instead of trying to beat them into submission. When it comes to the subconscious, all triumphs are Pyrrhic.

Most propitious mindfulness: Awareness of body, feelings, thoughts, and phenomena (the constituents of the existing world). It is easier for Westerners to think about mindfulness as presence, as being able to remain present and focused on what is going on inside and around them in the present moment.

Most propitious concentration: This is single-mindedness, defined as wholesome one-pointedness of the mind, as being able to unify the mind and concentrate on a single object with little wavering. This is how we learn to still our minds and gain peace and equanimity. Our minds are like restive puppies: we must learn how to tame them or they will run amok. Strengthening our ability to concentrate and focus on things that are important is conducive to happiness. The polar opposite is attention deficit disorder. I have never heard anyone say, "I have ADD (or ADHD), and it makes me really happy!" Taming and harnessing the mind is always advantageous in the long run.

The Buddha's Four Noble Truths and Eightfold Path are a prescription to alleviate suffering. No god or religion is referenced anywhere in them. In addition, the concept of "taking refuge" in the Three Jewels of Buddhism has always made sense to me.

Three Jewels of Buddhism

Taking refuge in the Buddha: This means taking refuge in our "Buddha nature," the fact that we were born with human consciousness and have the ability to become awakened, something obviously impossible without human consciousness.

Taking refuge in the dharma: This simply means to take refuge in the Buddha's teachings, to study and try to learn various aspects of his teachings.

Taking refuge in the sangha: *Sangha* means "community." Again, the number one thing correlated with happiness is the quality of our intimate relationships. For eons humans lived in tribes just like most mammals. In our society many people feel alienated and estranged from any particular communities. In our cities, it is very easy to live a life that consists of working for money eighty hours a week and then collapsing at home in front of the television. With so many people being diagnosed with clinical depression, maybe it is time to look at our society and examine why workers feel so disconnected — as Karl Marx predicted they would when they do not directly enjoy the fruits of their labors but instead work on assembly lines producing things for people they do not know. Loving, supportive communities are an essential part of the Buddha's teachings.

The problem with the way mindfulness is currently taught in America is that it is detached from the broader philosophy and psychology. When you secularize these meditative processes and remove them from their paradigms, then the emphasis is placed on attaining temporary states of calm rather than healing your life. And that is why so many misguided meditation teachers inaccurately speak about brains when they should be talking about minds, because they are ignorant of the Buddha's teachings and are trying to justify this one practice outside of its original paradigm with pseudoscience or scientific-sounding mumbo jumbo.

Simply put, the second noble truth is that the root of all of our suffering is desire. Desire manifests positively as clinging and negatively as aversion. The mind attempts to cling to and prolong joyous feelings and avert and squash painful feelings. For me, being authentic in this context relates to being present. The past is gone and the future does not yet exist, but our minds seem to ping-pong between these two nonexistent poles. Pain does not cause suffering; pain, when it occurs, is just information — information about something that needs immediate attention. But trying to avert pain, rejecting information about something that needs immediate attention, causes suffering. As mentioned in chapter 3, if your arm is broken, the pain signals your mind to stop thinking about your honeymoon in Hawaii or what you will have for dinner and focus on getting your arm fixed. Period. Life is replete with joys and sorrows. Each particular feeling is ephemeral, so trying to cling to joys that will wane, or trying to avert inevitable pain, causes us frustration and disappointment. It causes us to suffer. And if we learn to practice mindfulness, we find that the antidote to most of what ails us — the mind's clinging and aversion — is authenticity: being present, nonreactive, nonjudgmental, and compassionate.

Many of our reactions that we consider completely normal are actually maladaptive. Many of our instantaneous reactions to stimuli can make matters worse. For example, I live in Los Angeles and must drive on highways and freeways quite often. I have seen countless racing drivers cut off other drivers without even signaling, and the slighted drivers instantaneously react with cursing, honking, and the requisite middle finger. Even though there is less road rage now and fewer people are being shot on highways than there were years ago, it is maladaptive and potentially life-shortening to engage in such reactive behavior. Moreover, the racing driver could be rushing his pregnant wife to the hospital to give birth or hurrying to another emergency. And yet very often our minds do not consider all possibilities — many people take it personally when someone cuts them off. The Buddha taught "skillful means," that we must be the ones who say, "This type of behavior stops with me. I will not pay my suffering forward. I am going to break this chain of unskillful solutions, of maladaptive reactions."

Our minds are designed to learn from the traumatic experiences of our childhoods and to construct prejudgments to keep us alive and safe. And we know that this has worked, because we are alive! However, all of those subconscious fears and prejudices from years and years ago (if you espouse attachment theory, then they began in the first days, weeks, and months of our lives) are hindering us from being authentically present — from fully focusing our consciousness on what's occurring in the present moment. And when we cannot "be here now," as Ram Dass would say, this implies that traumatic memories from the past, and expectations of potential future suffering, may also be hindering us from being as authentically vulnerable and loving as we want to be in relationships.

Buddhism today is best regarded as a prescription to help us alleviate the suffering our minds inadvertently create when they try to prolong ephemeral pleasure and avoid inevitable pain. Recognizing this leads to insights into how to reconstruct the notion of authenticity that we deconstructed in chapter 1: learning to be present, or "be here now." Chapter 9 offers an even more powerful tool to help us clean up our prejudices and be present: at-onement.

Chapter 9

The Square Peg/ Round Hole Syndrome

Artists and musicians have been attempting to convey their visions of the divine since time immemorial. In 1948, Barnett Newman displayed a numinous, monolithic painting titled *Onement*, which I believe relates to the words *oneness* and *atonement*. At-onement, or *atonement*, is a rich and important word that will help us reconstruct the notion of authenticity that we deconstructed in chapter 1.

At-onement, atonement — atONEment — occurs when we realize our inner essential wholeness (as we discussed in chapter 7 regarding Advaita Vedanta), despite our minds' usual insistence that we are not good enough, that we can do better, that we can do more, that we will be happy at some time in the future when we accomplish or attain something, that we would have better lives now or be happier if certain events had not transpired in our childhoods, and so on. As noted earlier, meditation and yoga from the Hindu lineage were designed to allow us to (temporarily) feel whole, to enable us to taste the nectar of wholeness, the wholeness that is synonymous with being 100 percent present, with focusing clearly on the present moment and not allowing our minds to remember or regret phenomena that occurred in the past, or to plan, fantasize, or fear phenomena that may or may not occur in the future.

In that presence, which most people experience only in glimpses, we can realize our Higher Self, our true nature, and, in a spiritual sense, experience "authenticity." This is the real gift of any spiritual practice: to feel ease and eschew dis-ease and the unease that the mind creates, if only for a moment. And the lovely part about tasting the nectar of inner wholeness, of inner perfection, of oneness, of stillness, is that it can inspire us to make healthier choices throughout our stressful days. Twentieth-century Zen master Shunryu Suzuki once told his students: "Each of you is perfect the way you are... *and you can use a little improvement*." Whatever part of us has the ability to observe our thoughts without reacting to them, as if we are watching passing clouds, is our perfect part, the part that is whole and "good enough." *Why not?* Do you have an alternative? Do you have an explanation for the thousands of cogitations that run through our minds daily? The doubts? The fears? The impostor syndrome that so many people suffer from (and which I discuss in chapter 10)? Can you explain the incongruence between what we consider to be our (rarely revealed) inner selves and "the faces we prepare, to meet the faces that we meet," as T. S. Eliot called the facades we present to each other in "The Love Song of J. Alfred Prufrock"? Do you have another narrative for why our minds seemingly run amok for most of our waking hours and cause us stress, anxiety, and depression?

Unless we are complete narcissists, our minds — the thousands of mostly redundant and negative thoughts that we experience every day — could use some improvement (and if we are narcissists, then our minds could probably still use some improvement, but we simply would not realize or admit it). Whatever we consider to be the watcher of our thoughts I equate with our Higher Self. Try it on for size while we discuss at-onement, even if it sounds airy-fairy to you. If we are "born-again atheists" then we can think of those watchers as "Mystery" or "what we do not know that we do not know." If we are theists then we can think of it as Brahman, nirvana, moksha, God, Jesus, sunyata...it actually does not matter. As long as you recognize that you have thoughts, rather than you are thoughts.

Our minds are just the operating systems or software that run the hardware. As previously stated, Descartes put our culture on a misguided trajectory when he made thinking the premier attribute of existence. Instead of "I think therefore I am," it would be psychologically healthier to believe "I breathe therefore I am" or "I observe therefore I am." Getting our personal identity by means of the hamster wheels in our heads is an accident looking for a place to happen.

So now we have parsed the distinction between thinking and the part of us that observes our thoughts and we employ daily practices such as yoga and meditation to temporarily taste our essential oneness and wholeness; however, to truly realize our Onement or Oneness, we must learn how to "clean up" and/or "reframe" our pasts so that we can be as authentic as possible in the present moment. Or...how to survive your childhood now that you're an adult.

Here is how to do this: first, we must understand that, in an effort to keep us safe, our minds make judgments. Judgments began in childhood when whatever we experienced as traumatic caused our minds to say, "Wow! That was really embarrassing, humiliating, shameful, physically painful, frustrating, upsetting, disappointing, threatening, heartbreaking . . . *I am never going to let that happen again!*" In an attempt to prevent more embarrassments, pains, frustrations, and disappointments from ever happening again, our minds created judgments, prejudices.

But the past is dead and gone, and our stories are all that remain of those events that marked our consciousness. Unfortunately, our stories often contain judgments. The way we choose language to create our narratives speaks volumes about our prejudices. For example, on January 6th, 1985, I was a passenger in a car that skidded on a wet road into the blunt end of a guardrail. The guardrail pushed the engine of the car through the passenger seat and out through the back window. An impact wound to the left side of my face required a great deal of reconstructive surgery over the course of two years. If you saw a photo of what remained of the car, you would agree that it is difficult to imagine how I survived. For twenty-five years after the car accident, when people approached me and asked, "How did you get that scar?" or "What happened to your face?" I replied, "I was almost killed in a car accident."

I ended up taking a transformational course (not unlike the ones I now teach), during which we wrote the stories of our lives and then recounted them to partners aloud. Our partners were tasked with "deconstructing" our stories — separating what actually occurred from the language we chose to describe it — to make the reconstruction of whatever happened as accurate as possible. When I said, "I was almost killed in a car accident," my partner replied, "No, you weren't." I explained to him: "My face was smashed off of my skull, my femur was shattered into hundreds of pieces (which usually pierce the femoral artery, causing the person to bleed to death in fifty seconds), the hospital refused to notify my parents because they did not think

I was going to live...trust me: *I was almost killed in a car accident.*" "No, you weren't," he reiterated. Finally, he corrected me: "You were in a car accident. There was a car accident. *Everything else you added.*" "Almost killed" is like "almost pregnant." You are either pregnant or you are not; you are dead or you are not. And suddenly, after twenty-five years, I realized that adding the words *almost killed* contained a judgment. And that judgment was: "This should not have happened," because having your face blown off your head when you are eighteen years old is traumatizing. However, sucking everyone into my "woe is me" drama for the following twenty-five years, subconsciously trying to obtain sympathy, framing it as victimhood in an unjust world, was keeping the car accident alive in my mind. I wanted something I could not change to be different. Telling a story of judgment and resentment for twenty-five years was unintentionally disempowering. It was inauthentic. "There was a car accident." Period. My face is what it is. Not accepting my past and my face and who I am resulted only in perpetuating my own suffering.

What I needed to learn was a new or altered definition of the word *forgiveness* that related to the concept of at-onement, atonement. For me, forgiveness means reframing our unchangeable pasts to eliminate the resentments that our minds create, in order to release our prejudices, stop our suffering, and show up for every present moment as authentically and nonjudgmentally as possible.

Worse, unforgiveness is our desire to share our suffering. Think about this for a moment: "Resentment is like poking yourself in the eye and waiting for someone else to go blind." Even if someone committed a heinous act, if we are unwilling to forgive him or her, then our subconscious desire is to pay our suffering forward. That is a hard pill to swallow, especially when we live in a culture where the concept of justice is based on the code of Hammurabi, also known as "An eye for an eye." But as the saying goes: "An eye for an eye leaves the whole world blind." Does our sense of justice mean reciprocity of feeling? Do we need to make certain that the perpetrator knows how bad he made us feel by killing our child, and must we do this by killing his or her child? Paying our own suffering forward is what the Buddha would refer to as an "unskillful solution."

There is no blame here. It is completely pointless to blame parents, schools, capitalism, science, religion, or society. What we want is new ears for new music, a new understanding of human consciousness, some new insights into our current paradigm regarding justice, and a new understanding of forgiveness/atonement so that we can address a new understanding of authenticity. Childhood is traumatic. *Especially for children.* Children want to be loved and they have to learn discipline so that they can become "productive members of society." We raise children the same way we tame pets in our culture — with carrots and sticks, rewards and punishments. We deny them mother's milk, force them to sleep alone, make them eat when they are not hungry and sleep when they are not tired. Nietzsche's most famous adage, "What does not kill me makes me stronger," seems to have influenced at least a few generations of parents preparing their two-year-old babies with enough self-discipline to eventually get them accepted at top-tier universities and have the best opportunities for succeeding at the American dream.

In chapter 3, I proposed that depression and suicidal ideation can be read as people tacitly saying, "I was not loved in the manner I should have been loved as a child — namely, *unconditionally.*" It is depressing to grow up with so much pressure to succeed by someone else's measure of success that now you wish to kill yourself. Agreed. But instead of killing yourself or taking antidepressants, try forgiveness, atonement, acceptance. After attending a compassion seminar at UC Berkeley with Rick Hanson and Fred Luskin, I decided to try forgiveness. Twenty-five years after being the passenger in the aforementioned automobile accident, I located the driver of the car (on Facebook, of all places). And after what turned out to be an extremely lengthy and gut-wrenching dialogue about exactly what had transpired on the night of January 6th, 1985, I was able to utter the words "I forgive you." This did not mean I condoned his behavior. This did not mean I wanted to be friends with him. It meant I released my right to resent that the car accident occurred, that I was ready to ask for my freedom.

"Pain is unavoidable; suffering is optional." Pain does not cause suffering; it is the mind's intolerance of pain that creates and prolongs our suffering. A car accident is what it is. An accident. The driver of the car did not wake up that morning and think, "Today I will try to kill Ira Israel." *Accident.* Sure, I could spin it so I am a victim or hero, but both are inauthentic. And if we want authenticity, then we learn to accept pain when it is occurring, and learn not to allow our minds to resent it afterward, because it is the resentment that makes us suffer.

Forgiveness does not mean condoning someone else's behavior. Forgiveness means releasing the resentment about past events that we cannot change. Every time we hear judgments — as in "This should have happened instead" or "That should not have happened" — it means we are not accepting things we cannot change. If our best friend were sitting on the sofa trying to shove a square peg into a round hole, we would try to stop her — wouldn't we? Let's think of our minds as our best friends. By resenting past events, we only cause our own suffering. Nobody is asking us to condone someone else's behavior. We do not even have to contact anyone else. We need to find rituals that allow us to explore the resentments our minds have created — we can even go so far as to thank those resentments for keeping us safe all these years — and then figure out ways to release them. Try closing your eyes and imagining the face of someone whose actions harmed you. Hold the image for a few seconds, and then say the words "I forgive you."

What grudges have you been harboring? How often do you hear "woulda-coulda-shoulda-didn't" ring in your head? "I should not have gotten married so young." "I should not have gone to law school." "I should have gone to law school." "My mother was borderline and so were my first two husbands — what are the chances of that happening? I must be some kind of magnet for borderlines!" "My parents should not have gotten divorced." "My pet dog should not have been hit by a car." "My best friend should not have gotten cancer."

- Who do you need to forgive in order to show up authentically today?
- When will you be ready to forgive everyone you resent, including yourself?
- What do you need to do to release the fears and prejudices your mind created during your childhood, so that you are free to be truly present for your adult life and relationships?

This is atonement: realizing your inner wholeness and releasing the resentments that cause your own suffering. Whenever you are ready to stop suffering, simply release the resentments and judgments that your mind has created.

Chapter 10

How to Own Your Life

What if I forgave myself? I thought. What if I forgave myself even though I'd done something I shouldn't have? What if I was a liar and a cheat and there was no excuse for what I'd done other than because it was what I wanted and needed to do? What if I was sorry, but if I could go back in time I would not do anything differently than I had done? What if I'd actually wanted to fuck every one of those men? What if heroin taught me something? What if yes was the right answer instead of no? What if what made me do all those things everyone thought I should not have done was what also had got me here? What if I was never redeemed? What if I already was?
—— CHERYL STRAYED, *Wild: From Lost to Found on the Pacific Crest Trail*

On this perfect day when everything is ripening and not only the grapes are becoming brown, a ray of sunshine has fallen on my life: I looked behind me, I looked before me, never have I seen so many and such good things together. Not in vain have I buried my forty-fourth year today; I had the right to bury it....How could I not be grateful to the whole of my life?
—— NIETZSCHE, *Ecce Homo*

A bumper sticker states, "It is never too late to have a happy childhood." Another paradox in a cascade of paradoxes obscuring the truth. And yet, in this book I have been asking that we test our intellectual comfort zones in order to shift our paradigms and perspectives. The level of consciousness that created a problem will be unable to fix it, according to Einstein. We need new levels of consciousness; we need to see things in new ways, to embrace apparent paradoxes. Our level of consciousness creates resentments and judgments about the past in a futile effort to stave off inevitable future pain. This makes it challenging for us to be truly present, to be authentically in the present moment and temporarily — *or maybe permanently through atonement* — shed our fears and prejudices. *Why not?* Why does this seem so far-fetched? Is it possible that being awakened is synonymous with being present, with focusing on what is occurring in the present moment and not allowing our minds to drag us back into the unchangeable past or forward into an imaginary future?

To our minds, a glass of water is either half empty or half full. The glass of water is what it is. We are the ones who label it half empty or half full. The human prefrontal cortex is designed to categorize phenomena in a binary manner: black and white, good and bad, short and tall, good and evil, empty and full. But reality "out there" is what it is. Half full or half empty, good or bad, all depend on our perceptions. And it is within our power to reframe our perceptions. Particularly about our childhoods. Letting our minds tell us things "should" have been different — *things we cannot go back in time and change* — is an absurd waste of time. Wishing we could change something we cannot is a resentment. And resentment is like drinking poison and waiting for someone else to get sick. We cause only our own suffering. Rather than bitch and moan about the distance between reality and our expectations about how reality should have been, we need to ask ourselves what we need to do to clean up our stories about our entire pasts, including our childhoods. Because our stories probably contain judgments that tell people about our expectations rather than convey an accurate portrayal of our pasts.

On the other hand, before we try on some new phrasing, let me introduce one more paradox: I believe that all children should say their parents did the best they could, and that all parents should tell their children that they, the parents, could have done better. If parents tell their adult children: "We did the best we could as parents," they inadvertently invalidate the children's experience of childhood. It tells them: "We did the best we could, so if you are not psychologically perfect, then it is your fault, not ours." Though it is not intended to further wound the child, saying "We did the best we could" to your child is narcissistic and lacks empathy. Even if parents did the best they could (and of course they did — only a psychopath would make an effort to be a lousy parent), it is offensive to say it to your own children. However, children actually should tell themselves: "My parents did the best they could" (even if their parents were abusive, emotionally withholding, demeaning, suffered from Munchausen syndrome by proxy, pressured them to get good grades or be religious, or did not know how to attach and connect in a loving, positive manner). Specifically, although we may have learned inferior attachment skills from our primary caregivers, it is of no benefit to blame them for anything. Blaming parents, siblings, and other caregivers is just another resentment. We may disagree with the choices they made, we may not be able to condone their behavior, but now that we are adults we are 100 percent responsible for who we are and whatever wounds we need to heal.

Please try this "owning your life" exercise on for size: find a mirror, look into your own eyes in the mirror, and say the following to yourself:

- I am supposed to be me.
- I am supposed to look exactly as I look.
- My life is supposed to be exactly the way it is.
- My childhood was supposed to transpire exactly as it transpired.

This act of "owning your life" — embracing every single moment that has transpired because every moment contributed to your being exactly who you are today — is a way to release all of your mind's resentments. And it is the psychological culmination of everything discussed in this book. "Owning" who we are, including our childhoods and everything that brought us to this present moment, simply means radically accepting reality and "giving up all hope of having a better past."

And once we have stopped being victims of the stories our minds created, we can decide which daily tools — gratitude, loving relationships, helping others, healthy living, exercise, authentic communications, meditation, eating correctly, being in nature, and so on — will give us our adult version of "the good life." The main tool we are going to explore here, to help us be as authentic as possible, is congruence. Let's spend a few moments deciding who we should be and how we can make our outer worlds congruent with our inner worlds. For example, we might decide the following:

- I enjoy life more when I am involved in an intimate relationship.
- I need to spend more time in nature, hiking, surfing, and sitting on park benches.

- I am going to make an effort to live a more balanced life.
- I love expressing myself through art, dance, theater, music, writing.
- I have outgrown some of my friends.
- I need to make amends with…
- I need to communicate more authentically with…
- The way I earn money would be more fulfilling if…
- I need to figure out a way to make my relationships more harmonious.
- I need to stop stressing myself out by rushing around — it is okay to relax.

As I mentioned in chapter 8, we are fairly myopic as a species. We tend to think in terms of months — mortgages, rent, credit card bills, and so on — when it may behoove us to think otherwise. For example, the average human lives 27,375 days. How many days old are you today? Statistically, is your life likely more than half over, and you are still complaining about things that happened 20,000 days ago? Conversely, even if you have another 20,000 days to go, have you already planned what you would like it to say on your tombstone? As previously discussed, wanting our tombstones to read "Beloved, Loving Husband" or "Beloved, Loving Wife" or "Beloved, Loving Father" or "Beloved, Loving Mother" or "Beloved, Loving Sister" or "Beloved, Loving Brother" exponentially increases our tolerance around our loved ones. We need beacons. We need long-term goals. Long-term goals help guide the daily choices we make. Isn't it time we committed ourselves to having more compassionate, loving relationships?

If we want to be grateful about our finite existences, all we have to do is pick up a newspaper and read about the scores of people who became nonexistent today, many of whom did so unexpectedly (although whether it is better or worse to be conscious that death is imminent is debatable).

If we let our minds go on autopilot they tend to run amok. The point of the initial chapters of this book was to make us conscious of the many assumptions that we consider "normal" and to persuade us to question the realities that we create. Once we can see the realities we have unintentionally created, then we can consciously decide who we want to be — that is, set an intention — and match our actions and our way of being to those intentions. Sometimes, who we know we are and should be, and the facade we choose to show the world, are vastly different. For example, if we do not want people to objectify us sexually, then we should not dress sexily; if we do not want people to want to hang out with us only because we have money, then we need to stop offering to pay everyone's tab. We must learn who we are, know who we should be, and be that person.

If we suffer from the impostor syndrome — meaning that deep down we are terrified that people will find out we are a fraud and will humiliate and leave us — then we need to learn congruence. Our culture has a narrow bandwidth for emotions; we need to cultivate real relationships in which we can feel free to express ourselves and not be judged. This is one of the ways psychotherapy works. I am not suggesting that all relationships be therapeutic, but that we avoid relationships with people who show their love for us by relentlessly judging and criticizing us.

Moreover, our society embodies a zero-sum mentality originating from the concept of "survival of the fittest." Even though human beings have the technology to produce and distribute enough food to feed everyone on earth, many people will go to bed hungry tonight. Such competition was extremely useful when there were limited resources, but now that we can create abundance, we must learn to choose compassion over competition. Hoarding or wasting does not make sense.

Similarly, we know that ego gratification is fleeting and that the mind is akin to a hedonic treadmill. Our long-term goals, then, must include loving relationships rather than more property ownership that, for most people, entails more debt and more stress. When given the choice, we must choose love over ego gratification. No sane person wants it to say "He Was Right" on his tombstone. We want it to say "Beloved" and so must make our daily actions and interactions with others fall in line with that goal.

Finally, there is little long-term benefit in seducing people into liking our facades. Many people come across like walking billboards or résumés. Listing our accomplishments when we meet people does not engender the kind of loving relationships that we truly crave. We must choose authenticity and authentic communications instead of the one-upmanship that many of us engage in when we are conducting busyness/business. I am not advising you to march into your boss's office and show your authentic self, but I suggest that we all spin our stories less. "There was a car accident" sounds much different than "I was almost killed in a car accident." Now that we are adults, we are responsible for our way of being in the world — the way we stand, talk, sit, look at others, dress, choose subjects to discuss, and so on. Let's consciously choose who we want to be and then make our way of being as congruent as possible with what we have decided.

Chapter 11

Cultivating Authentic Connections

I discuss attachment theory in detail in chapter 2 because how we learned as children to connect and attach to others strongly influences our happiness as adults. Moreover, these dynamics are dynamic (ha-ha), meaning they are like muscles we can choose to exercise and make stronger or let atrophy. We can choose to lean in or to avoid others once we understand all facets of whatever relationships we are dealing with.

Attunement is how we connect face-to-face with other people — through eye contact, facial expressions, the proximity of our flesh to theirs, our gestures, our energy levels, even the pheromones and smells that do not usually rise to the conscious level. How we attune to another person is analogous to how instruments in a symphony are tuned to the piano before a concert. And, by the way, in one sense this is also how psychotherapy functions: quite simply, by *not* invalidating the patient's emotional experience. For example, in normal conversation you might say, "It's going to rain later," to which someone might add: "*But* it will clear up tomorrow." So yes, the two of you arrive at the truth regarding the weather for the next twenty-four hours, but the dialectic through which it is accomplished invalidates one person's emotional experience. Attunement is when we seek to connect with others on a non-verbal level. In the weather example, if the second person had said, "*And* it will clear up tomorrow," the two people would have arrived at the truth without any emotional invalidation. Language creates reality, so we must be conscious of this when we choose to respond to people with "Yes, but..." rather than "Yes, and..." Often people conduct conversations as if they are trying cases in front of the Supreme Court: they want to be right; they want to win the conversation, which is awesome if they are in court. But when they are at dinner with a loved one, there can never be one winner and one loser in a conversation — just two losers.

We yearn for connection, and yet many of us learned to create drama in order to feel allowed to express our (supposed) authentic selves. Drama functions like fire under a petri dish, allowing us to distill pure emotions. But drama also pushes people away. As adults, we now need to learn to express ourselves compassionately and as authentically as possible. If it is time to improve our conversational skills and create a more loving and positive reality, then let's become conscious of the words and actions we choose in order to express who we are, who we want to be, and what type of lives we want to lead.

If we believe that language affects the way we perceive reality, the way we cogitate, the way we interact with others, and the way we communicate, then if we cannot or do not live up to our word, we forfeit many privileges, such as expecting other people to honor their agreements with us. How many times would you let someone show up an hour late to a scheduled meeting before asking that person why he thinks that his time is more valuable than yours? Some people live by the creed that their word is their bond, and if they say that they are going to do something or be someplace at a particular time, then they do everything in their power to make that happen. Others take a while to learn that they can bounce only so many verbal checks before their credit is revoked and nobody will invest in them.

Let's take a look at the way people communicate in the twenty-first century. We know that 95 percent of communications are nonverbal, so how has technology affected our relationships? Text messaging may seem wonderful for the occasional brief note to reschedule a meeting, but it often engenders ambiguity and confusion by failing to convey essential nuances such as disappointment, hope, irony, sadness, and elation. Texting is a terrible means of communicating emotions, WITH THE POSSIBLE EXCEPTION OF TEXTING IN CAPITAL LETTERS (a.k.a. shouting) — LOL! — DUH! — sideways smiley faces, and multiple exclamation points!!!!!!!!!!!!!!

I have witnessed countless patients lose important relationships over miscommunications caused by texting and what I call "subtexting." Subtexting is the implied information given and the rampant misinterpretation of that information — namely, the response time between text messages. When we stand in front of a fellow human being and look into his or her eyes, we get a tremendous amount of information, and we receive that information in real time. When we speak with someone on the telephone, we can hear his or her breathing and the timbre, rhythm, and tone of his or her voice, and we get a sense of what that person's current disposition or emotional state is. Are they frantic, discombobulated, out of sorts? Or are they serene, calm, composed, lucid, empathetic, and thinking clearly? All of this is lost when texting. You have no idea if the other person is sitting on the toilet, driving furiously, high on crystal meth, massaging their wrists with a razor, having sex, in a yoga class, or having a meltdown. During every second that we wait for a response, our minds try to assemble visual scenarios of the other person's current reality from the pixelated characters of the text message and the time it takes for the other person to respond. We wonder, "Is my husband really shopping, or is he chatting with a pretty cashier?" "Is my son safe or was he hit by a bus?"

I am not sure what the etiquette is where you live, but in Los Angeles it has become moderately acceptable to "ghost" someone, which is when someone slowly stops returning your messages and you end up, like a frog being boiled alive, scalded by the silence. As Marshall McLuhan said, "The medium is the message." All new technologies are exciting, but if we do not quickly comprehend their limitations, then they may end up being more detrimental than helpful. In this case, I strongly advise people to avoid answering open-ended questions in text messages and to text back "When is a good time to speak?" to arrange a telephone or face-to-face conversation.

I consider my iPhone a frenemy. In fact, I have implemented my own strict etiquette for text messages, and I usually make very specific requests: I ask people to please text me only to arrange telephone conversations or face-to-face meetings, or to report unexpected emergencies with a note such as: "Running late. Sorry." I have witnessed so many people have entire one-sided, passive-aggressive conversations and implode like Jon Favreau in *Swingers* that I feel confident in advising people to avoid anything that resembles a conversation via text message.

Human beings need physical contact — we need to see into other people's eyes. This interaction does not transpire via text messaging. One hug equals one million text messages. Posting on Facebook, Instagram, Twitter, and Snapchat deludes us into believing we are engaging in relationships. But nobody is ever going to receive a pat on the back through a video screen. We need contact, we need to break bread with other human beings, we need touch, we need to practice the dying art of conversation, we need empathy, love, and compassionate speech. Authentic face-to-face interactions are how we heal the attachment wounds of our childhood (and they probably create new neural pathways, too!).

Texting subconsciously reinforces avoidant behavior that results in alienation and distance, and I believe it correlates strongly with the rise in depression over the last twenty years. In five hundred years, when historians look back on our society, I believe they will correlate the increase in cases of clinical depression to the rise of social media. I have never heard of a patient going into a psychotherapist's office and saying, "I feel truly loved, supported, and appreciated by my friends, family, coworkers, and loved ones...*and I am depressed*." Compassionate, empathic, face-to-face interactions are where the healing of emotional wounds takes place.

To that end, here are two transformational tools/exercises that I suggest you try in order to raise the bar on your intimate relationships immediately: reflective listening and Marshall Rosenberg's "nonviolent communication."

Reflective Listening

We all know how to listen. But how many of us know how to make another person feel heard? There is a profound difference between passively listening to someone and actively mirroring that person and letting him or her know that you are tracking what he or she is expressing, and that you understand and empathize with whatever he or she is feeling. The best tool for this, by far, is reflective listening, because it forces people to become attuned to the other person's emotional experience. If you want to truly connect with another person and make him or her feel heard, here is how you do it: reflect back what this person is saying with the same "affect" (the same facial expression and overall demeanor and pitch) that he or she employs. So if they are staid, then your face is staid; if they are smiling, then you smile to the same degree; if they are frowning, then you frown, too. This mirroring of facial expressions subconsciously validates the other person's emotional state, whatever he or she is feeling at that moment.

Next, notice how long or short, and how deep or shallow, the person's breathing is and try to replicate it. Do your best to synchronize with his or her inhalations and exhalations. Once your faces are physically attuned and your breathing is paced, look him or her in the eyes (in my office, I also have couples hold hands) and "reflect" back whatever the person says. The speaker can start with short phrases — fifteen to twenty words or fewer. Very simply, the reflector looks the speaker in the eyes and says, "So, if I hear you correctly, you are saying that..." and then repeats back whatever the speaker said in the same tone as precisely as possible. Most importantly, it is best to leave the concepts of right and wrong outside the room you are in, to be picked up when you leave. And as an incentive, remember Harville Hendrix's provocative question: "Do you want to be right, or do you want to be in relationship?"

When I am conducting this exercise with couples and they are attuned to each other and reflecting pleasantly back and forth, and right and wrong have been taken off the table, I have them tune in more deeply by reflecting nonsense sentences to each other, such as: "I see thirty-five green Martians dancing to 'La Cucaracha' on your head." After the other person stops laughing, he or she reflects back: "So, if I hear you correctly... you see thirty-five green Martians dancing to 'La Cucaracha' on my head." Then I tell them: "This is not about the content; this is about the process." Usually they then realize what it means to really connect with and attune to each other — beyond symbols on our phones, beyond spoken language beamed off satellites and hitting our ears through smartphones, and sometimes even beyond having simultaneous orgasms while in the same room. I try to really get people to connect with their partners on a nonverbal level — something that is completely impossible via text messaging or IMing.

We cannot go back in time and change our infancies and childhoods, and complaining about them only results in our own suffering. But as adults we can strengthen our attachment dynamics by learning how to truly connect with others on a physical level and tune in to whatever they are experiencing.

Nonviolent Communication

The best tool I have discovered for people to authentically express themselves is Marshall Rosenberg's nonviolent communication process. I have found that owning our own emotional experiences and communicating them without blame is the best way to inspire others to show up 100 percent for relationships and take responsibility for their own words and actions. If you are ever in a stalemate where you and a partner are pointing your fingers at each other, I suggest you try my version of Marshall Rosenberg's "4-Part Nonviolent Communication Process":

"I feel _____
[A FEELING]

when _____
[AN OBSERVATION ABOUT AN OCCURRENCE]

because I need _____.
[SOMETHING YOU NEED]

In the future would you please_____."
[A REQUEST]

"I" statements about personal feelings require people to be vulnerable, which attracts vulnerability and allows both parties to drop their defense mechanisms and be authentic. Conversely, blame only incites defensiveness. Usually the sentences in this exercise are worded like this: "I feel hurt/sad/disappointed/frustrated when you don't respond to my text messages within four or five hours, because I need reassurance about our relationship. In the future would you please return my text messages in a timely fashion?"

For more information, please read *Nonviolent Communication: A Language of Life*, part of the Nonviolent Communication Guides series by Marshall Rosenberg, and visit www.cnvc.org.

I hope this chapter on attunement has raised your consciousness about how you connect with others verbally and nonverbally. We are interdependent creatures, and we establish those connections, as well as trust and security, through how we express ourselves. Reflective listening and nonviolent communications are hands-on tools that enhance the way you connect with and attach to others. We need to take responsibility for the way we present ourselves, so that we attract the authentic love that we crave.

Here's a model that inspired me: Nietzsche thought we should construct our lives as if we were constructing a great work of art. He wrote,

One thing is needful. — To "give style" to one's character — a great and rare art! It is practised by those who survey all the strengths and weaknesses that their nature has to offer and then fit them into an artistic plan until each appears as art and reason and even weaknesses delight the eye. Here a great mass of second nature has been added; there a piece of first nature removed — both times through long practice and daily work at it. Here the ugly that could not be removed is concealed; there it is reinterpreted into sublimity. Much that is vague and resisted shaping has been saved and employed for distant views — it is supposed to beckon towards the remote and immense. In the end, when the work is complete, it becomes clear how it was the force of a single taste that ruled and shaped everything great and small — whether the taste was good or bad means less than one may think; it is enough that it was one taste!

It is the "style" that we create, our way of being in the world — without blaming others, without complaining, without becoming reactions to our parents or things that occurred during our childhoods that we cannot change, and with adult intentional discernment, not juvenile judgment — that will help us attract the love and create the lives that our hearts truly yearn for.

Conclusions

If your daily life seems poor, do not blame it;
blame yourself that you are not poet enough to call forth its riches;
for the creator, there is no poverty.
—— RILKE

There is no plan B. The only possible panacea is authenticity, which is difficult but must be attempted and practiced on a daily basis. It is up to us to break the chains of unskillful solutions that were handed down to us, to consciously decide who we want to be, what type of relationships will nourish us, and what type of world we care to live in. "We are the ones we have been waiting for," writes Alice Walker. Nobody is going to shed our fears and prejudices for us. Nobody is going to have personal integrity and be authentic if we do not inspire them to do so. Making commitments to engage in healthy practices (such as meditation and yoga) and being congruent and having our outer lives match our inner lives — or, more specifically, deciding our long-term intentions and having the discipline to follow them every day — will keep us at the higher end of our happiness spectrums.

In chapter 1 we explored the possibility that we can only be authentic when we talk about ourselves and decry our own inauthenticities. In chapter 3, I argued that the past is gone (yes, I realize that is redundant), and that the only thing keeping our childhoods alive is our stories about whatever transpired — and very often those stories contain resentments that only result in our own suffering. I asked rhetorically, "What is the point of complaining about things that you cannot change?" Your way of reacting against your childhood is inauthentic: if you desire to be rich because you grew up poor, that is inauthentic; if you want to play tennis at an exclusive country club because your parents forced you to grow up in an anarcho-syndicalist commune, that is inauthentic; if you stay a virgin because your parents were promiscuous, that is inauthentic. We emulate the characteristics of the caregivers we had when we were young as a way of trying to retroactively subconsciously gain their approval and love; and we also subconsciously incarnate the opposite characteristics as a way of individuating from them and becoming our own selves. Becoming something in order to gain approval is inauthentic; being reactive and rebelling against something is also inauthentic.

What I specifically advocate seeking is a new definition of authenticity that encompasses attachment, atonement, attunement, presence, and congruence:

Attachment: It is best for us to be aware of our primary attachment style. Our internal barometers were shaped before we could speak, and they either informed us that the world is an inherently scary place with finite resources, or told us that it is a loving place of abundant resources (or that it occupies some gray area in between). Our way of being in the world, our core issues, and our dispositions may be influenced subconsciously by our initial experiences, but if we can get a glimpse of our patterns and what lets us feel comfortable connecting with others, then we can make healthier long-term decisions. We need to be aware of our attachment styles to get the love we truly crave as adults.

Atonement: Wanting something in the past to have transpired differently is an absurd waste of time and energy. It is impossible for anyone but us to unbetray us, to unabandon us — to figure out a way to heal our core emotional and psychological wounds. Our childhoods were traumatizing and we created our way of being in order to survive them and do our best to get our emotional and psychological needs met at the time. But now those same childhood defensive mechanisms may be hindering us from being authentic in our adult relationships. Not accepting that something we cannot change happened only results in our own suffering. We need to find rituals that will let us say good-bye to the stories our minds created that are laden with prejudices and resentments. Forgiving everyone unequivocally is the way we scrub the resentment out of our stories.

Attunement: Being able to attune to other people and make them feel as if whatever they are experiencing is valid will make all our relationships better. This interaction does not transpire via text messaging. We need contact. We need hugs. We need long, relaxed meals with enthusiastic and stimulating conversations about subjects other than work. We need connections with other human beings, and we want those connections and attachments to be secure, trustworthy, positive, supportive, loving, and healthy. Human beings do not grow or evolve in bubbles. We are interdependent creatures. And we live in a society that inadvertently foments separation, competition, and alienation, so we must continuously be attaching and attuning to others in order to attract the compassion, love, and support that we want and need.

Presence: The future is a void. Our minds create resentments about the past and project them into imagined potential future scenarios in a futile attempt to stave off or at least be prepared for possible traumatic surprises. This defense mechanism, which was essential to surviving our highly competitive and often disappointing and frustrating childhoods, is now hindering us from being authentic in the relationships that are integral to our lives and our healing journeys. We must learn how to observe the mind's incessant leaps into possible future scenarios and gently correct it by teaching it to be present.

Congruence: Listening to our tastes and our Higher Selves to glean information about why we are alive, and then deciding what we should do during the brief time we are alive...keeping our facades, which we present to others, in alignment with our beliefs: that is congruence. *Living by other people's rules and other people's measures of success is a surefire path to frustration and disappointment.* We need to learn how to mitigate our own hypocrisy. We need our way of being in the world to match our core beliefs, not our core wounds.

So, if you want to know "how to survive your childhood now that you're an adult," then learn how to surf apparent paradoxes, learn how to be present, learn how to embrace every moment of your life hitherto, learn how to "own" and accept who you are today, learn how to shed your fears and prejudices, learn discipline, know what your attachment style is and how to improve it, know what your remissions are and do not let them become afflictions or addictions, learn how to attune to other people so that you can securely connect with them, and accept the fact that our futures are uncertain, and that when they occur they will certainly contain both joys and sorrows.

Acknowledgments

Larry Payne attended my first lecture in Los Angeles and subsequently called Cheryl Fraenzl at the Esalen Institute. Cheryl hired me to teach "Cultivating Meaning and Happiness through Mindfulness and Yoga" workshops, but more importantly it was at Esalen that finally I found my tribe of fellow caring, compassionate, educated seekers actively trying to make the world a better place. While teaching and studying there, I have had the privilege of breaking bread with some of the greatest living thought-leaders, including Sam Keen, Michael Murphy, Warren Farrell, and Linda Bloom, the last of whom introduced me to Georgia Hughes at New World Library. And that is how this book made it into your hands.

The longer narrative includes my psychotherapy internship under the tutelage of Gilbert Newman, who taught me not only cutting-edge therapeutic interventions but also how to be an adult and how to be a man. During the time spent working with Gilbert in Berkeley, I was privileged to study at Spirit Rock with Rick Hanson, Fred Luskin, James Baraz, Phillip Moffitt, David Richo, and Jack Kornfield. Before that I was blessed to study Eastern philosophies and spiritualities with

Alan Wallace, David Gordon White, Barbara Holdrege, and the late Ninian Smart while in graduate school at University of California, Santa Barbara. During my undergraduate years at the University of Pennsylvania I studied Western philosophies under the guidance of Alexander Nehamas and Philip Rieff.

Since 1992 I have practiced yoga and meditation with hundreds and hundreds of teachers in Rishikesh, Koh Samui, Bali, Paris, London, Manhattan, Santa Barbara, Los Angeles, Oakland, Austin, Berkeley, San Francisco, Lake Tahoe, Palm Springs, Raleigh, and Chicago. Rodney Yee, Richard Rosen, Govind Das, Guru Singh, Jerome Mercier, Tracee Stanley, Malachi Grieves, Noah Levine, and Sigrid Matthews inspired me deeply with their dedication to these practices.

For all of their support, patience, and tolerance over the past thirty years, I must thank Theodore Kyriakos, Jeff Faski, Antonia Perensky, Sherri Brooks, Robert Lusson, Rachel Bargiel, Michelle Friedman, Darryl Marks, Josephine Wallace, Amanda Mills, Felicia Tomasko, Cassandra Brennan, Alexandra Geneste, Dorothy Gibbons-White, Michael Sibay, Emmanuel Itier, Irving Schwartz, Howard Spector, Natalie and David Jones, Shannon Byrnes, Jasmin Palmer, Heather Davis, Donna Goldman, Cathy Bitton, Gregory Lambertie, Julia Apostle, Barbi Steinhilber, Ruth Sullivan, Marcia Hyman, Jai Uttal, Anne Brochet, Gill Holland, Rob Lefko, Ted Jackson, Ron Alexander, Melinda Flannery, Jerilyn Hesse, Jennifer Jaffe, Donald Altman, and Dr. Edward Ines and his amazing staff.

Besides towering intellectuals such as Adèle Van Reeth, Slavoj Žižek, Paul Fry, and Mark Blyth, who have expanded my consciousness, there are many artists, musicians, filmmakers, and writers whose work has sparked my sense of wonder. Above all, in the 1980s maestro Riccardo Muti made symphony tickets available to Penn students for two dollars, so I thank him for opening up an entire universe to me. Next I must humbly thank all of the strangers at the tables next to me in cafés in Paris and the East Village who recommended books and films to me. Lastly but not leastly, big thanks to the musicians whose work has provided me continual joy and solace: Peter Gabriel, Daniel Lanois, Sting, Van Morrison, Elvis Costello, Patti Smith, Morrissey, Ani DiFranco, Joan Baez, Joni Mitchell, Richard Thompson, Kate Bush, Leonard Cohen, Lloyd Cole, and all of the jazzheads who teach me that I still have so much to learn.

Notes

Introduction

Page 2, *Over 20 million Americans take antidepressants*: According to the *Guardian*, "Like other countries, the use of antidepressants in the US has soared. In 1998, 11.2 million Americans used these drugs. By 2010, it was 23.3 million." Mona Chalabi, "Antidepressants: Global Trends," *Guardian*, November 20, 2013, www.theguardian.com/news/2013/nov/20/mental-health-antidepressants-global-trends.

Chapter 1. What Does It Mean to Be Authentic?

Page 14, *scientific paradigms shift every generation*: Thomas S. Kuhn, *The Structure of Scientific Revolutions* (Chicago: University of Chicago Press, 2015).

Page 18, *"The whole of life would be possible"*: Friedrich Wilhelm Nietzsche, *The Gay Science: With a Prelude in Rhymes and an Appendix of Songs* (New York: Vintage Books, 1974), 297.

Page 19, *there are 121 suicides in America every day*: American Foundation for Suicide Prevention, "Suicide Statistics," afsp.org/about-suicide/suicide-statistics. The article cites 44,193 suicides per year, which I divided by 365 to come up with 121 per day.

Page 21, *children develop "false selves"*: D. W. Winnicott, "Ego Distortion in Terms of True and False Self," in *The Maturational Processes and the Facilitating Environment: Studies in the Theory of Emotional Development* (New York: International Universities Press, 1965).

Chapter 2. How to Avoid Being a Professional Child

Page 27, *when a baby is initially held up to a mirror*: Jacques Lacan, "*Le stade du miroir, comme formateur de la fonction du Je,*" in *Ecrits 1: Texte Intégral* (Paris: Seuil, 1966).

Page 30, *what is known today as attachment theory*: John Bowlby, *Attachment and Loss*, vol. 1: *Attachment* (New York: Basic Books, 1968).

Page 31, *experiments known as "the Strange Situation"*: Mary Ainsworth and John Bowlby, *Child Care and the Growth of Love* (London: Penguin Books, 1965).

Page 34, *when a baby is put down alone for the first time*: Arthur Janov, *The Primal Scream* (London: Garnstone Press, 1973).

Page 39, *"Happiness cannot be pursued"*: Mick Brown, *The Spiritual Tourist: A Personal Odyssey through the Outer Reaches of Belief* (New York: Bloomsbury, 1999), 3.

Page 39, *"There are two tragedies in life"*: George Bernard Shaw, *Man and Superman* (1903; reprint, Cambridge, MA: University Press, 1905), 174.

Page 39, *ranked as the thirteenth-happiest in the world*: Josh Hrala, "The World Happiness Index 2016 Just Ranked the Happiest Countries on Earth," Science Alert, March 17, 2016, www.sciencealert.com/the-world -happiness-index-2016-just-ranked-the-happiest-countries-on-earth.

Page 39, *most human beings who ever lived*: Ken Dychtwald, in a lecture at Esalen, November 12, 2016.

Page 39, *767 million of our fellow human beings*: World Bank, "Overview," last updated October 2, 2016, www.worldbank.org/en/topic/poverty /overview.

Page 40, *"marshmallow test"*: Walter Mischel, *The Marshmallow Test: Mastering Self-Control* (New York: Little, Brown, 2014).

Page 44, *"If you think you're enlightened"*: Ram Dass, Facebook post, November 28, 2013, www.facebook.com/babaramdass/posts/66500845 6864556.

Chapter 3. Your Mind: A Resentment Factory

Page 57, *$4,078 in credit card debt*: Kimberly Amadeo, "Average Credit Card Debt: U.S. Statistics," The Balance, updated June 15, 2017, www.the balance.com/average-credit-card-debt-u-s-statistics-3305919.

Page 61, *"We are not mad, we are human"*: Leonard Cohen quoted in Ira Nadel, *Various Positions: A Life of Leonard Cohen* (New York: Vintage, 2010).

Chapter 4. The Myth of Romance

Page 63, *romantic love as we know it today*: Denis de Rougemont, *Love in the Western World*, trans. Montgomery Belgion (1963; repr., Princeton, NJ: Princeton University Press, 1983).

Page 63, *romantic love is not conducive*: Robert A. Johnson, *We: Understanding the Psychology of Romantic Love* (San Francisco: HarperSanFrancisco, 1999).

Page 66, *what they [lovers] need is not*: de Rougemont, *Love in the Western World*, 42.

Page 66, *"Romantic love is the single greatest energy system"*: Johnson, *We*, xi.

Page 68, *"When a man's projections on a woman"*: Johnson, *We*, 108.

Page 68, *sexual intercourse in America has become*: David Schnarch, *Constructing the Sexual Crucible: An Integration of Sexual and Marital Therapy* (New York: Norton, 1991).

Page 69, *"how can you desire what you already have?"*: Esther Perel, "The Couples Conference 2015" lecture, Manhattan Beach, CA, April 25, 2015.

Page 70, *eight years, the average lifespan of marriages that end*: Rose M. Kreider and Renee Ellis, "Number, Timing, and Duration of Marriages and Divorces: 2009," *Current Population Reports*, US Census Bureau, May 2011, www.census.gov/prod/2011pubs/p70-125.pdf, 15.

Chapter 5. Taking Care of Busyness

Page 76, *"Finance has increasingly made us creatures"*: William N. Goetzmann, *Money Changes Everything: How Finance Made Civilization Possible* (Princeton, NJ: Princeton University Press, 2016), 2.

Page 76, *the national average for a mortgage is $222,261*: LendingTree.com, "What Does the Average Home Owner Pay on a Mortgage?," Daily Real Estate News, January 3, 2012, RealtorMag, realtormag.realtor.org /daily-news/2012/01/03/what-does-average-home-owner-pay -mortgage.

Page 76, *Our government has borrowed $19.8 trillion*: Wikipedia, "National

Debt of the United States," en.wikipedia.org/wiki/National_debt_of_the_United_States.

Page 77, *"Mindful Revolution"*: Kate Pickert, "The Mindful Revolution: Finding Peace in a Stressed-Out, Digitally Dependent Culture May Just Be a Matter of Thinking Differently," *Time*, February 3, 2014.

Page 82, *working an average of forty-seven hours*: Jena McGregor, "The Average Work Week Is Now 47 Hours," *Washington Post*, September 2, 2014.

Page 82, *Americans have the least amount of vacation time*: Robert B. Reich, *Supercapitalism: The Transformation of Business, Democracy, and Everyday Life* (New York: Vintage Books, 2008).

Page 83, *average American spends four minutes a day*: Ruth Whippman, *America the Anxious: How Our Pursuit of Happiness Is Creating a Nation of Nervous Wrecks* (New York: St. Martin's Griffin, 2017).

Page 83, *making us feel alienated and alone*: Robert Putnam, *Bowling Alone: The Collapse and Revival of American Community* (New York: Simon and Schuster, 2007).

Page 83, *"A man is a success if he gets up"*: Jonathan Cott, *Bob Dylan: The Essential Interviews* (New York: Simon and Schuster, 2017).

Page 84, *Steve Jobs and Bill Gates would not have become*: Malcolm Gladwell, *Outliers: The Story of Success* (New York: Little, Brown, 2008).

Chapter 6. How to Blow Off Steam and Keep Your Life Manageable

Page 87, *a "wall of separation between church and state"*: Thomas Jefferson, *Jefferson's Letter to the Danbury Baptists* (January, 1, 1802).

Page 89, *"There is no female Mozart"*: Camille Paglia, *Sexual Personae: Art and Decadence from Nefertiti to Emily Dickinson*, vol. 1 (New Haven, CT: Yale University Press, 1990), 247.

Page 89, *they are the "sterile animal"*: Friedrich Wilhelm Nietzsche, *Beyond Good and Evil: Prelude to a Philosophy of the Future*, trans. Walter Kaufmann (New York: Random House, 1966), 89.

Page 93, *"A remission too severely constrained"*: Philip Rieff, *My Life Among the Deathworks: Illustrations of the Aesthetics of Authority* (Charlottesville: University of Virginia Press, 2006), 12.

Page 103, *"We do not receive wisdom"*: Marcel Proust, *Remembrance of Things Past* (Harmondsworth, UK: Penguin Books, 1983).

Chapter 7. What Are You Doing on Planet Earth?

Page 111, *"born-again atheist"*: Gore Vidal, *At Home: Essays, 1982–1988* (New York: Vintage, 1990), 235.

Page 114, *children who remembered their past lives*: Ian Stevenson, *Twenty Cases Suggestive of Reincarnation* (Charlottesville: University Press of Virginia, 2002).

Page 117, *she found that people who have* jobs: Sonja Lyubomirsky, *The How of Happiness: A Practical Guide to Getting the Life You Want* (London: Piatkus, 2010).

Page 118, *our culture's faith in a Christian God*: Friedrich Wilhelm Nietzsche, *The Gay Science: With a Prelude in Rhymes and an Appendix of Songs* (New York: Vintage Books, 1974).

Page 119, *scientific paradigms shift every generation*: Thomas Kuhn, *The Structure of Scientific Revolutions* (Chicago: University of Chicago Press, 2015).

Chapter 9. The Square Peg/Round Hole Syndrome

Page 134, *"Each of you is perfect"*: Shunryu Suzuki, quoted in David Chadwick, ed., *Zen Is Right Here: Teaching Stories and Anecdotes of Shunryu Suzuki, Author of* Zen Mind, Beginner's Mind (Boston: Shambhala, 2007), 1.

Page 134, *"the faces we prepare"*: T. S. Eliot, *The Love Song of J. Alfred Prufrock* (Toronto: McClelland and Stewart, 2016).

Page 138, *"What does not kill me"*: Friedrich Wilhelm Nietzsche, *Twilight of the Idols; or, How to Philosophize with a Hammer*, and *the Antichrist*, trans. R. J. Hollingdale (New York: Penguin Books, 1968), 23.

Chapter 10. How to Own Your Life

Page 145, *the average human lives 27,375 days*: Joshua Kennon, "The Average Person Lives 27,375 Days. Make Each of Them Count," July 14, 2012, www.joshuakennon.com/the-average-person-lives-27375-days-make-each-of-them-count.

Chapter 11. Cultivating Authentic Connections

Page 152, *"The medium is the message"*: Marshall McLuhan, *Understanding Media: The Extensions of Man* (Cambridge, MA: MIT Press, 2013), 1.

Page 154, *"Do you want to be right"*: Harville Hendrix and Helen Hunt, *Making Marriage Simple: 10 Truths for Changing the Relationship You Have into the One You Want* (New York: Crown Archetype, 2013), 66.

Page 157, *"One thing is needful"*: Friedrich Wilhelm Nietzsche, *The Gay Science: With a Prelude in Rhymes and an Appendix of Songs* (New York: Vintage Books, 1974), 232.

Conclusions

Page 159, *"We are the ones we have been waiting for"*: Alice Walker, *We Are the Ones We Have Been Waiting For: Inner Light in a Time of Darkness* (London: Weidenfeld and Nicolson, 2007).

Index

abortion debate, 87
action, right (most propitious), 126
Acton, Lord, 78
Adam and Eve myth, 65
addictions, 97, 100–101, 163
ADHD, 16, 40
Advaita Vedanta, 109; consciousness and, 120; Hindu concepts related to, 113–18; history of, 112; main concepts of, 110–11; meditation and, 110, 113; nondualism and, 112–13; yoga and, 110, 113
Ainsworth, Mary, 31–32
alcoholism, 59
ambivalent attachment, 32, 33
American dream, 2, 79–80, 81, 85, 124. *See also* hedonic treadmill
American Foundation for Suicide Prevention, 19
America the Anxious (Whippman), 83
anal sex, 96
Animal House (film; 1978), 91
antidepressants, 2
anxiety, 40; diagnoses of, 17

architecture, 89
Aristotle, 94, 97
Arjuna (Hindu mythological figure), 117–18
art, 89, 94, 145
assumptions: about romantic love, 70–71, 72; attachment style development and, 29–30; awareness about, 3, 109; language and, 9–10; of Western civilization, 10
atheists, 71, 111, 120, 135
Atman (Higher Self), 20, 111, 113, 120
at-onement/atonement, 131; authenticity and, 161; defined, 133, 140; forgiveness and, 137–40; meditation/yoga and, 133–34; negative thoughts and, 134–37; reframing the past for, 135–37
attachment styles: authenticity and, 33, 160–61; caregiver interaction and, 34–36, 143; consciousness of, 36, 109, 160–61, 163; development of, 29–32, 143, 149; types of, 32–34

175

About the Author

Ira Israel is a Licensed Professional Clinical Counselor and Licensed Marriage and Family Therapist. He graduated from the University of Pennsylvania and holds graduate degrees in psychology, philosophy, and religious studies. Ira is the creator of the DVDs *A Beginner's Guide to Happiness, A Beginner's Guide to Mindfulness Meditation, Mindfulness Meditations for Anxiety*, and *Mindfulness for Urban Depression* and leads "Cultivating Meaning and Happiness through Mindfulness and Yoga" workshops at the Esalen Institute and throughout the United States.

For more information, please visit www.IraIsrael.com.